# SHARPEN YOUR
# POSITIVE
# EDGE

## SHIFTING YOUR THOUGHTS FOR MORE
## POSITIVITY & SUCCESS

# TINA HALLIS, PH.D.

Hallis, Tina
*Sharpen Your Positive Edge: Shifting Your Thoughts for More Positivity & Success,* by Tina Hallis


Editing by Holly Henschen, www.HollyHenschen.com
Book Design by Kendra Cagle, www.5LakesDesign.com
Back Cover Photography by Sarah Sandell
ISBN-13: 978-0-9984718-1-5
Library of Congress Control Number: 2017909585

**Learn more about Tina's programs and products at:**
**ThePositiveEdge.net**

# What People Are Saying

Since August of 2013, I've shared positivity tips in my weekly newsletter and on my website, **www.ThePositiveEdge.net.** This book is a collection of some of these tips and is meant to be a resource for increasing your positivity, and ultimately, your quality of life. Here's what some of my newsletter readers have to say about how the weekly tips have made a difference for them.

*"As a recovering pessimist, I appreciate Tina's tips on how to stay positive. I know the importance of positivity, but can easily slip back into negative thoughts. The tip gives me a boost, and a reminder to stay positive, as I begin my week."*

—**Cory Erickson,** President & Chief Executive Officer
Career Momentum, Inc.

---

*"When I read (Tina's) tips, I am instantly moved to smile, which starts off my day with a great mood. When I am having trouble throughout the day, I reflect back on past tips to help motivate me to stay positive."*

—**Bridget Kimbro,** Deposit Operations Specialist

---

*"I read Tina's tips every time I see one in my inbox. They are relatively short and always contain practical advice I can immediately put into practice in my life. I highly recommend them and feel confident they will help you become a more positive person!"*

—**Brian Uderman,** Professor and Director of Online Education
University of Wisconsin-La Crosse

*"I have enjoyed the tips because they are a breath of fresh air in a time when there is anger and frustration everywhere. We all need to spread hope, positivity, and kindness wherever we can."*

—**Amy Esry,** Human Resource Consultant

---

*"What I love about (Tina's) tips is that:*
- *They are written in a simple language.*
- *They point to immediate practical application.*
- *They contain personal anecdotes or experiences.*
- *They make me pause and reflect on the realities of today's common problems facing humanity."*

—**Mahesh Pamnani,** Founding Partner, Trainer and Chief Happiness Officer, Inspire2Aspire Consulting, Hong Kong

---

*"The tips provide me with hope, a better understanding of myself and others, and guidance in times of need."*

—**Adrian**

---

*"Life is a challenge in itself and then you throw in an 8-10 hour work day for most people . . . We all need to use a guide such as yours to learn how to live in the now and enjoy every minute of every day, no matter what environment we are in. Enjoy and appreciate getting up every morning, getting ready, enjoy the ride to work and the beautiful sunrises and the scenes, the work day itself, the people you work with and deal with, the ride home, and the evenings spent with family, friends, pets, or whatever . . . somehow we have to learn how to make it all a positive experience. I believe a journal with your tips and thoughts would help to make it a daily routine or culture."*

—**Elisa M. Rollo,** Vice President of Deposit Operations

*"I like reading positive thoughts first thing in the morning because it helps me stay positive all day long; they help me stay in the present moment and not dwell on the past. I like the thought-provoking tips that let me say I am doing well and stay in gratitude."*

**—Teresa Dalhoe Bednarski**

---

*"I feel it's human nature to head in the direction of negativity and it takes a much more conscientious effort to find and focus on the good. I need daily reminders (sometimes multiples if I'm having a rough day!) and I like that your tips are a quick, easy read. Plus, you provide them in stories that are often relatable. I also appreciate that you give action items—it's not enough to say "just think like this"—giving tools and ideas that help readers take action in that direction is much more useful."*

**—Jennifer Hanson,** Vice President of Operations

---

*"The tips are practical and real and give me a positive jolt in a way that coffee cannot!"*

**—Karen Miyoshi,** Program Manager II

---

*"The tips help put things in perspective and to sort out emotions. I find they give insight to understanding others better, as well as ourselves."*

**—Christina,** Finance Manager

---

*"Every Monday when I get to work, the first thing I do is read the tip Tina sends from The Positive Edge. I can always relate it to something I have done or will be doing, or need to do. And it puts me in a positive frame of mind to begin my workweek on the right foot. Sometimes later in the week, I go back and re-read some of my favorites to help keep me on track."*

**—DeeAnna Deane,** Human Resource Manager, Training Specialist

*"Your tips are thought-provoking and often it's your perspective that causes me to take a different viewpoint. This is the enlightening and exciting aspect! There is always a more energizing way to contemplate the challenges in life and the vehicle you provide with your words more than achieves this."*

**—Adrienne Ansley,** Resource Teacher and Workplace Coach ,
New Zealand

---

*"I look forward to the tips Tina sends every week as a source of comfort, insight, and inspiration; they remind and help me to  sharpen my attitude skills."*

**—Bob A.**

---

*"I enjoy the tips as they help me to reflect and think about all of the goodness in my life and why it is important to be positive. Her tips are one of the few that I actually read on a regular basis. The length is great (short and focused), and the content is something that I can use immediately."*

**—Janet Nodorft,** CWC, CWWS, MS, Blue Jewel Coaching

---

*"The biggest benefit that I've been reaping from your messages is to stop wasting energy on negative brain talk and save that energy and use it for doing good things for others, or thinking positive thoughts, or making my life easier/more fun. If I'm not thinking about helping others, something positive, or making my life easier/fun, then I tell myself to stop and redirect my energy into one of those three things."*

**—Heidi**

# Contents

Section 3:
# BUILDING POSITIVE RELATIONSHIPS

Section 4:
CREATING POSITIVE GOALS

# Introduction

## *Life can be hard*

Let's be honest. Life can be hard. Work can be hard. There can be challenges or uncertainties in our health, finances, relationships, and jobs that overwhelm us and stress us out. There can be situations that are frustrating and upsetting. Sometimes it may feel like the waves of life are crashing down on us. No wonder we can spend so much time focused on all the problems, the things we don't like, and the stuff that just isn't fair! If the challenges are related to our work, pretty soon we can't remember why we even wanted this job or the purpose of our work. It can make us feel miserable, poisoning every part of our lives.

I've been there. Like all of you, I've had situations in my life that spiked my stress level, and some sent me into a downward spiral of negativity. I've had people that have made me feel betrayed or manipulated. At work, I've had jobs, bosses, and projects that I didn't like. Some were frustrating because I felt I couldn't use my strengths or add value. A few felt pointless or boring. Some left me feeling overwhelmed.

What if I told you that there *is* another way, we *can* have more enjoyable days and even a higher quality of life with more success? I'm not talking about making major changes in your lifestyle or career. I'm talking about taking small steps to shift your *thoughts* using practical, everyday strategies and insights from the rapidly expanding field of Positive Psychology.

## *We can change*

Until the late 1990s, the scientific community believed that once we became adults, our *brains stopped changing.* The wiring was set, and we couldn't really modify our thinking. But new studies and technology have shattered that paradigm.[1] An influx of recent research explores how our brains do continue to change and how our very *thoughts* impact those changes. This natural tendency of our brains to rewire is called neuroplasticity, which can be influenced by both external *and internal* factors.

What do these new findings mean for you and me? That we have the power as individuals to create a different perspective. We can physically rewire our brains to see our work and lives in a more positive light. We can reduce our stress and increase our peace and happiness. We can use our minds to change our brains for a better life. Now that's exciting science!

There isn't a catch, but there is a challenge. It takes effort to notice our thoughts and to choose what we focus on. It's easier to let our thoughts go where they will. Most of us don't realize it, but our natural tendency is to dwell on all the bad things around us, in our past, and that might happen in the future.[2]

This strong negative bias is actually important. It's a by-product of evolution's gift to help us survive and keep us safe. As a species, we had to get really good at noticing potential dangers and remembering anything bad that happened so we could be prepared to take action. If things were good, our brains could ignore it. No action necessary! But today, we have far fewer life-and-death situations compared to our ancestors, so we need a better balance.

The great news is that insights and strategies from Positive Psychology are showing how we *can* work towards achieving this balance and make it easier to override our natural negative thoughts. A multitude of studies by researchers like Barbara Fredrickson, Martin Seligman, Sonja Lyubomirsky and many others are finding that a variety of practices and approaches can help us get better at noticing the good. These practices physically change our brains and reinforce our more positive mindset, which not only improves our daily life, it increases our motivation, productivity, and resilience! No wonder greater positivity has been found to lead to greater success.[3]

## *Try this exercise*

When it comes to our quality of life, here's something more to consider. We don't experience the world—we experience *our thoughts* and *think* it's the world. Here's a simple exercise that drove this home for me.

Take a moment to think of something that drives you crazy about your job or life. Find something specific that's totally frustrating and irritating—something you wish you could change. It could be a person, a situation, a project, etc. Hold that thought for a moment. Close your eyes and let the feeling sink in. Now, imagine that tomorrow morning, this is the first thought that enters your mind as soon as you wake up. This negative thought is there, at the forefront of your mind, every spare moment all day.

What kind of day would that be? How would it affect your mood—your reaction to other things throughout your day? I've had some people say, "That would suck!" Others have said, "That *is* my day!"

I don't want to leave you feeling this way, so now please think of something you *like* about your work or life. Focus on something specific you really appreciate or enjoy. Again, it could be a person, a situation, a project, a work-benefit at your company, etc. Take a moment to hold that thought, close your eyes, and let the feeling sink in. Now, imagine that tomorrow morning this *positive* thought is the very first thing that enters your mind. And all day tomorrow, this is what you focus on, every spare moment. How would this day be different? The same things happen, but you have a different focus.

If you take the time to *feel* the difference, you get a glimpse into just how powerful our thoughts can be. They not only impact how we view our work, but also how we view our relationships, our lives—even ourselves. If we want to have more enjoyable days, a better work experience, and more wellbeing, all we have to do is change the way we think!

My goal is to make these choices and changes easier for as many people as possible. That's why I've written this book: to serve as a toolbox so you can experiment with a variety of strategies to see what works for you. We're all different, with different genetics and lifestyles, so my favorite practices may not be a good fit for you. The only way to find out is to try a few and see how they feel.

## *More than just theory*

These aren't just some interesting theories and concepts I've read about. These are life-changing insights and techniques that I've experienced first-hand. In 2012, I was laid off from my job as a scientist after 11 years with my company. That was stressful enough. Then, I decided to start my own business, The Positive Edge, instead of looking for another job. A year ear-lier, I had discovered Positive Psychology. I was fascinated and excited to find a science focused on how we can all improve our lives by increasing our positivity! Based on my experience, if there's one place we could use this information, it's at work. So I started reading and learning as much as I could, trying to figure out how to share this amazing research with my coworkers. I took being laid off as a sign that I should spread my message beyond my former company.

The next couple of years brought waves of uncertainty and fear as I tried to figure out how to build a company and reinvent myself as a speaker and trainer. Was I crazy? It took a few months before the waves of nausea sub-sided. Actually, I wonder how other people survive such huge changes and doubt without having the tools I had learned from Positive Psychology. They were critical in helping me manage my stress and fears. I'm incredibly grateful that I had so many powerful strategies to get me through those tough times.

I've now spent more than five years learning and reviewing this ground-breaking science. Of course, I still use the insights and tips I've learned every day. Life is always good at supplying us with what I call "rich material"—opportunities to practice staying positive. It gets easier over time, but the journey never ends. The path just gets a little smoother and less bumpy.

## *The purpose of this book*

I frequently speak, train, and write about increasing our positivity. But I want to reach more people and provide another format geared towards helping busy people like you and me remember and *apply* these concepts. Information alone does not improve our lives—we need to actually use it to see a change.

*Information applied to a situation causes transformation.*

That's how the idea for this book came to be. It's a toolkit with a selection of short, practical, and easy-to-use strategies and tips you can apply in your daily life. The tips are organized by category with a table of contents to make it easier to find the ones that can have the biggest impact for you and your current situation. So instead of reading them in numerical order, skip around and use the tip that fits the moment. Read it and reflect on how you could use it in your own life. What other ideas does it bring to mind? What actions can you take? You can even take it a step further by discussing the tip with family and friends.

This book is *not* a daily calendar journal. You may find a strategy that you want to focus on for a week or more. You may pick a few at a time that are helpful for what's going on in your life right then. There may be some tips that you'll never use because they just don't fit your situation, or there may be some that you just don't like. There may be others you go back to again and again as a reminder. The key is that we're all different with different ideas, backgrounds, personalities, etc. The approach that works great for one person may not be a good fit for another. You have to experiment and find those tips that work best for you.

Once you choose one of the tips, it can be helpful to capture your thoughts by writing them in the space provided. Consider using the blank page to journal about examples, possible scenarios, or upcoming situations in your life where you could use these ideas. Feel free to record any and all thoughts that come to you. These reflections are always fun to go back and review weeks or months later.

If words aren't your thing, feel free to doodle or draw if it helps you think or is your way of collecting your thoughts. You don't have to write anything at all to benefit—choose what works for you.

You'll notice that some of these strategies have similar themes. I've found that encountering a related message again, but with a slight twist, can suddenly give me new clarity and understanding. My intent is not to be redundant, but to provide multiple opportunities for new ideas to stick.

My hope is that this book will make it easier to bring more positivity into your life so you can enjoy more peace, happiness, and the kind of success you desire.

*Section 1:*

---

# INCREASING
# POSITIVITY

# 1. The Cascade of Giving and Receiving Kindness
*Pass it on*

I turned the key in the ignition of my car. Nothing! I tried again. With a sinking feeling, I realized that the battery was dead. I'd been sitting in my car because I had some time to kill between meetings. What I hadn't realized is that my lights had been on the whole time, and now my car wouldn't start. *And* my next meeting was in 15 minutes!

I got out and put the hood up. As I was searching for my jumper cables, an elderly man walked across the parking lot and asked me if I needed help. I told him my situation. He quickly retrieved a battery charger from his vehicle and attached it to my car. In a few minutes, my car was running. *Yes!* I offered to pay him, but he wouldn't hear of it. He was glad he could help.

How did that make me feel? I was incredibly grateful for his help and happy that I'd make it to my next meeting in time. Interestingly, as I went about my day, I noticed I was more eagerly looking for opportunities to do something nice for someone else (see Tip 28).

Studies show that receiving generosity and kindness increases the likelihood of extending generosity to others.[4] *And* kindness is likely to play an important role in setting a cascade of generosity in motion.[5] When we help others, we may not only be helping this one particular individual but potentially many others downstream.

What are some examples of people recently being kind to you? Of you being kind to others? What are some common situations where you could extend generosity to start a cascade?

## 2. Hugs from Grandma
*Savoring positive memories*

Although our brains naturally tend to remember the bad stuff, we don't have to be helpless victims to their negativity. We can change our emotions and attitudes by choosing what memory we want to focus on. I'm not saying it's easy, but there are tricks to make it easier.

One of my favorite strategies is to remember a time when we felt really loved, safe, or happy. Studies show that as we savor this memory, our bodies release chemicals that make us healthier and happier.[6] The more we can relive that moment using each of our five senses, the more real it feels.

I can remember sitting in my kayak in the middle of a beautiful lake in northern Wisconsin. The sun was setting, and I could see the colors reflecting in the calm water. I could hear the lonely call of loons, smell the fresh evening air, and feel the coolness on my skin. This is a favorite relaxing memory of mine.

Another wonderful memory that makes me feel safe and loved is to remember back when I was a little kid staying with my Grandma Vi (short for Viola). She loved to spend time in the kitchen cooking and baking. She would have her radio on, singing and dancing along to the music. I can still hear her singing "A White Sport Coat" with Marty Robbins in the background. I would sit at the table enjoying the smell and taste of her fresh bread with homemade strawberry jam or her warm molasses cookies. My grandma was so full of love for all the people in her life, but especially for her grandchildren. I can still feel her hugging me tight while making a sound like "Mmmm, mmmm," as if she was taking a bite out of her favorite food.

Grandma may be gone, but her love lives on in many hearts. Every time I pull up that memory to shift my thinking, I feel her hugs and love engulf me.

What memories can you dig up that create warm feelings? It could be a childhood memory, something recent, a place, a person, or just a special moment. Take time to savor and reflect on these memories, using all of your five senses. These are the real treasures in life!

_____

_____

_____

_____

_____

_____

_____

_____

_____

_____

_____

_____

_____

_____

_____

_____

_____

_____

_____

_____

_____

# 3. Life Lessons from a Warm Brownie
*Enjoy it before it's gone*

The brownies were fresh from the oven—still warm and fudgy and oh so yummy! I took little bites so I could savor the chocolatey flavor. These had to be some of the best brownies I'd ever had!

Suddenly, I realized I'd gotten distracted and had started thinking of the papers I needed to sort and file. I looked down at my plate. My delectable brownie was *gone*! I had missed out on enjoying those last bites . . . I felt sad and disappointed.

It's funny how right then it hit me—this is such a great analogy to how we live our lives. We get busy, distracted, caught up in what we need to get done next. There are so many things going on related to our work, household, family that it can be easy to forget to enjoy the moment. Then it's too late and the day is done, or the summer is over, or our kids have moved away, or our life is winding down. We don't realize how quickly the time is passing until something happens that makes us stop and reflect. It reminds me of this quote by the author Sidonie-Gabrielle Colette—"What a wonderful life I've had. I only wished I'd realized it sooner."

We don't have to wait until something is lost or ending to enjoy it now. We can find reminders to help us pause and savor. I like to use pictures or quotes in my office or on my bathroom mirror, file cabinet, or refrigerator. It could be a ring you wear or a special coin you keep in your pocket. Maybe it's a book, card, or poster that helps you pause and reflect.

What prompts could you use to remember to enjoy the moment before the moment's gone?

# 4.  Do You Rise and Shine?
*Setting your morning intention for a brighter day*

When you first wake up in the morning, and you're just remembering where you are and what day and time it is, what crosses your mind? Do you think about how tired you are or how you wish you could sleep more? Maybe your mind jumps to those things you're *not* looking forward to in your day—that stressful meeting, the bad weather, the irritating co-worker . . . If you're like most people, the strong negative bias of your brain can easily start you off with a less-than-positive outlook that sets the tone for your day. Thankfully, we have other options.

Here are a few suggestions to try. Set your alarm to go off five minutes before you need to get up. Spend that time thinking about things you're looking forward to or things you appreciate. See Tips 5, 7 and 16 for ideas on gratitude.

If it's hard to come up with ideas first thing in the morning, make a list the night before and put it next to your bed so you can read it when you get up. If that doesn't work, read over your list during breakfast or post a few notes on your bathroom mirror. The goal is to set a positive tone for our day with intention instead of letting our brains default to their usual negative focus.

I love my sleep. It seems like I'm always feeling warm and comfortable when the alarm goes off. It can be so hard to get out of bed in the cold and dark. When I remind myself of something I want to get done, something I'm looking forward to, or some of the things I'm thankful for, I find it energizes me and gets me moving with an upbeat attitude. Give it a try and see if you notice a difference.

Reflect on what you could think about before you get out of bed tomorrow morning. Keep the list by your bed and read it first thing when you wake up.

## 5. The Best Part of Getting a Cold
### *Practicing gratitude for your health*

Is there really anything good about getting a cold? When I have a cold, I have a hard time functioning. I can't breathe, my body aches, I have difficulty sleeping, and sometimes my throat is so sore that it hurts to swallow. I can't wait until I'm feeling better and not struggling to survive the day!

Yet, once I do feel better, I quickly forget how miserable I was and take my health for granted. I can remember many times when my husband would ask me if my cold was better. His question would make me pause and consider my stuffy nose or headache. Hmmm. "Yes," I would often respond, "I am feeling better today!" Without his question, I wouldn't have even noticed.

Humans are interesting creatures. We complain and hate feeling bad, but we can quickly get used to feeling good and may seldom remember to appreciate it. However, we can purposely reflect back and recall the misery of past aches and pains to remind ourselves how awful it was so we can enjoy our current wellbeing. For example, right now, in this moment, I'm sitting here feeling fine and breathing freely so I can appreciate the absence of a cold. Ahhhh! It feels good to feel good.

Some people have health issues, and they're constantly dealing with chronic pain or illness. Are they less likely to take the "good" days for granted? I haven't seen any studies on this, but I've certainly had friends and family who suffered from a major ailment and were determined to live life to the fullest and enjoy those days they were feeling better.

When was the last time pain or sickness was bothering you and making you miserable? Was it your back, joints, your stomach, maybe even a tooth? How does it feel right now? If it's better, use this moment as an opportunity to remember the discomfort and appreciate the fact that it's not hurting.

# 6.   Living in the Flourishing Zone
## *Improving your Positivity Ratio*

The Positivity Ratio is a concept from the work of social psychologist Barbara Fredrickson and others.[7,8] She's found that we need approximately three positive experiences for every one negative experience to flourish and enjoy the benefits of positive emotions.[9] Some of these benefits include more motivation, stronger resilience, better decision-making, and even better health. Interestingly, these positive and negative experiences that make up the ratio aren't just the external things that happen *to us*. They also include the internal experiences we *create* with our thoughts.

If we want to improve our Positivity Ratio, we have a few choices. Here are three examples:

- We can get better at **noticing** the good that's already there. Practicing gratitude in the moment is one option. Another is to reflect back on our day and look for the good things that happened.

- We can intentionally **add** good things to our day. These can be simple things such as listening to a favorite song, spending time with our pets, calling a friend, doing something nice for someone, taking time for a favorite hobby or pastime, etc. See Tip 17.

- We can **recall** a memory that makes us feel good. Instead of letting our minds instinctively dwell on some past negative situation, we can choose to remember something positive that happened recently or in the past. See Tip 2.

Studies show that the average American has a Positivity Ratio of around 2, which falls in the "OK" zone—we're getting by. The "flourishing zone" ranges from about 3 to 9.[8] When our ratio is low, we not only miss noticing the good things in our lives, we fail to see many of the opportunities and possibilities that exist because we're so focused on the negative.

What are some ways you could add internal and external positive experiences to improve your Positivity Ratio?

_____

_____

_____

_____

_____

_____

_____

_____

_____

_____

_____

_____

_____

_____

_____

_____

_____

_____

_____

_____

_____

_____

_____

_____

# 7. Gratitude and Chicken Guts
*Appreciating what you don't have*

When it comes to thinking about gratitude, it's common to reflect on those things we appreciate in our lives. But there are many twists we can take with gratitude. For instance, we can be grateful for things we *don't* have.

There was a time when I was a scientist at a chicken company. My job was to analyze the feed and the chicken meat. I vividly remember the few trips I took to the plant where they processed the chickens. As I walked through the cold, refrigerated building, I would see all these people standing at the conveyor belts, pulling out chicken guts by hand, hour after hour, day after day. The idea of handling dead chickens all day long in the freezing cold definitely made my job seem like a cakewalk. I was grateful I didn't have *their* job instead.

Now, don't get me wrong—I did not pity these people. I empathized with their complaints and, as I listened, it would remind me of all the good things in my work. I believe we can practice compassion *and* appreciation based on the many struggles people around us encounter. This idea can be controversial because we're told it isn't healthy to compare ourselves to others. However, I've found that in addition to feeling empathy for those who are dealing with challenges, I can also use it to find gratitude for things in my own life. I hope others can do the same with my challenges.

For example, when I'm feeling sick, it makes me really look forward to feeling better. And I hope it serves as a reminder to others around me to appreciate their health. When I was working as a scientist in Madison, Wisconsin, people would express concern over my hour-long commute. I told them this was my choice, but hopefully, it would also make them appreciate their 10-minute commute.

As you look around at other people in your life and in the news, what things, problems, and situations are you grateful that you *don't* have?

_____

_____

_____

_____

_____

_____

_____

_____

_____

_____

_____

_____

_____

_____

_____

_____

_____

_____

_____

_____

_____

_____

_____

# 8. Work-Life Balance Is Not a Noun
## *The action of positively balancing*

I sometimes get asked to speak on work-life balance. This is such a popular topic in a world where we're trying to do it all at work and at home. After all, with today's technology, shouldn't we be able to get more done in less time? Yet, now more than ever, many of us feel out of balance.

From my studies of Positive Psychology and my own experience, I've found that this balance is not something we can *find*. That's because we use words as if this balance were a noun when in reality it's an action verb. We cannot find balance because it's a continual action with ongoing adjustments, just like the tightrope walker who constantly moves his pole to keep from falling.

We like the idea of a magic formula that, if we knew it, our lives would suddenly become balanced and stay that way. Yet we all know there's so much fluctuation in each area of our lives that what's working for us now will likely not work next year, next month, or even next week.

My young daughter is helpful in reminding me about my need for balancing. She's very vocal about telling me when she feels we haven't been spending enough time together. "Moooooom! You're always busy, and we don't do anything fun together anymore!" This complaint is an obvious indication to me that I need to readjust my balancing. Other areas of my life that may need more attention aren't so easy to "hear." In an attempt to get more in tune, I've added this idea to my list of positive affirmations as a reminder to adjust the amount of time and energy I give to the different areas of my life as needed. (See Tip 78). My goal is to be more aware of the current situations with my work, family, physical health, spiritual health, friends, etc. This positive balancing is definitely an action verb!

Consider the different areas of your life right now. Do you need to make some changes to your positive balancing? Could you ask for help, delegate, or temporarily reduce your efforts in an area?

_____

_____

_____

_____

_____

_____

_____

_____

_____

_____

_____

_____

_____

_____

_____

_____

_____

_____

_____

_____

## 9. Could You Use a Vacation?
*Taking time off is good for you*

A while back, I was hiking around Valley of Fire State Park in Nevada. What a beautiful place! My family took a 10-day vacation that included visiting my parents in Phoenix and renting an RV so we could tour around southwest Utah. It's the longest family vacation we've taken since my daughter was born 11 years ago.

A common trend I noticed as we hiked through Zion National Park and Bryce Canyon is that most people were not speaking English. People from all over the world were enjoying the national monuments. Why were there so few people from the United States? Surveys show that Americans only use half of their paid time off (~10 vacation days and six holidays) and about 70% say they work while on vacation.[10] Some say it's because they feel guilty or they're afraid they'll be seen as lazy and be passed up for a promotion. Others say the work just piles up while they're gone. Workers in other countries take much more time off. People living in France, Germany, and Scandinavia routinely take as much as six weeks off every year.[11]

Studies suggest that taking more vacation reduces our risk of having a heart attack, and infrequent vacationing can increase our risk of dying overall.[12] Yet the current model of success and the culture at many companies have us working more hours and staying digitally connected to our work even when we're supposedly "off the clock." Research shows that we need to take a break and decompress so we can be at our best at work—and at home. Maybe we should ask if the life we're working so hard to create is fun to live?

When's the last time you disconnected and took a vacation? You don't have to travel far—just doing or seeing something different can be a great break. Reflect on how you might schedule a vacation of any length; maybe even just a couple of hours. What would you do? Where would you go? How would it feel to get away?

# 10.  The Positivity Payoff
*The benefits of focusing on the good*

I have to admit; there are times it can be really hard for me to notice the good stuff in my life. Sometimes it's just easier to sulk and let myself be upset, anxious, or feel down. It can seem like an impossible effort to break out of a downward spiral and shift my thoughts to something more positive.

And yet, I don't want to waste my life stuck in negative emotions. Not only do they take the enjoyment out of life, but they also hold me back from having the kind of life I want. My days are much better when I enjoy emotions like gratitude, joy, love, amusement, hope, serenity, and curiosity. *And* there are added benefits:[9]

- We think more clearly and make better decisions. For example, doctors primed to have a positive emotion are more accurate at diagnosing their patients' illnesses. Positively primed students perform better on exams.

- We more easily see the bigger picture. Studies show that people notice more of their surroundings and see more options.

- We are more creative. One study showed that people think of more uses for simple household objects when they're feeling a positive emotion.

- We are healthier and may even live longer.

- We recover from stressful situations more quickly both physically— decreased cortisol, blood pressure, and heart rate—and emotionally.

- We're more energized, which increases our motivation and productivity.

To be fair, negative emotions do serve a purpose—Check out Tip 37 for some of their benefits. Like many things in life, we need a balance.

Practicing positivity is like brushing our teeth—it doesn't last, so we have to repeat often. That's where the effort and practice come in.

Reflect on how these benefits could provide motivation for practicing strategies to stay positive. How could these benefits impact your life?

_____

_____

_____

_____

_____

_____

_____

_____

_____

_____

_____

_____

_____

_____

_____

_____

_____

_____

_____

_____

# 11. The Placebo Effect
*You get what you expect*

You don't need alcohol to get drunk—you just need to *think* you're consuming alcohol. You don't need a pain reliever to get rid of a headache—you just need to *think* you're taking a potent medicine. You don't even need a bronchial dilator to relieve your asthma—you just need to *think* you're using one.[13] And the list goes on, including not actually having knee surgery to feel better, but just thinking the surgeons repaired your knee.[14]

This phenomenon is called the placebo effect. It's incredibly powerful and has been considered a nuisance in clinical trials that are trying to prove the effectiveness of new drugs. But new research is being done to not only understand how this phenomenon works, but how we can harness its power.

Studies have uncovered that at least one of the underlying mechanisms is how our expectations impact our bodies' chemistry.[15] If we believe something is going to help us or hurt us—the "nocebo" effect—our physiology responds as if it's true. It might mean feeling better because we think we're receiving a helpful drug, or feeling bad because we think we're suffering side effects from the drug, even though it's just a sugar pill. Isn't it amazing how easily our brains are fooled?

Consider of how this translates to other parts of your life. If you think you can achieve something, your body prepares for and expects it. If you believe good things happen to you, your body prepares for and expects them. If you think you're going to fail at something or that nothing goes well for you, your body prepares for and expects it. It can become a self-fulfilling prophecy. Henry Ford captured this so well when he said, "If you think you can or if you think you can't, you're right." That's why it's important to pay attention to our thoughts and to find ways to catch ourselves expecting the worst.

Reflect on how the power of expectation affects your life. How can you make it work for you rather than against you?

_____

_____

_____

_____

_____

_____

_____

_____

_____

_____

_____

_____

_____

_____

_____

_____

_____

_____

_____

_____

_____

_____

_____

# 12. Using a Fake Smile to Boost Your Mood
*It's all in the eyes*

If you want to fool your brain into thinking you're in a good mood, all you have to do is fake a smile. However, it has to be the right kind of fake smile. If you only move your mouth and cheeks, it doesn't work. The trick is to make sure you also crinkle the corners of your eyes.

Psychologist, Richard Davidson at the University of Wisconsin–Madison, and others have found that certain parts of the human brain are activated by different emotions. Because of this brain mapping, they can see which areas light up when we're happy.

In one study described in Davidson's book, *The Emotional Life of Your Brain,*[16] volunteers were told to smile using just their cheek muscles as researchers monitored their EEG (electroencephalogram that monitors brain waves). The results showed that electrical activity in the brain wasn't significantly different from the baseline activity.

Then researchers asked participants to smile with both their cheek *and* eye muscles. Only when *both* muscle groups were used did they see a greater activation of the region in the brain associated with happiness.

What I love about this fantastic research is that you can try it for yourself. Right now, try smiling with just your mouth and cheeks. Hold for 5-10 seconds. Now *also* crinkle the corner of your eyes so you're using the muscles around your eyes. Hold for 5-10 seconds. I find when I include my eyes, the smile starts to feel real, and pretty soon it's easier to keep smiling because I feel happier.

When could you use this technique in your day? Try it when you're in different moods, such as feeling neutral, slightly down, or anxious. When does it work best for you?

# 13. Want to Know the Secret to Success?
## *It's already inside of you*

I was in shock! The head of R&D at the biotech company I was working at wanted *me* to join his team and to promote me from a senior scientist to a manager! Me!! I finally had the courage to ask him why. He said it was because I was skilled at getting along with everybody and he needed more of that on his team. He also said I was good at keeping an upbeat attitude. I couldn't believe it! I didn't see these things as anything special. It's just the way I was.

We all have our own special talents and gifts that make us unique, but because they're part of us, we can have a hard time seeing them as anything special. Understanding and using our talents can make a big difference in our lives, helping us to become our best selves. Not sure of your gifts? Here are some tips for doing a little detective work.

- Ask a friend, "What am I good at? What are my talents?" Give them some time to think about it.

- Think of a situation or project that brought you great satisfaction and happiness. What were you doing? What made it so enjoyable?

- Take a personality or strengths test. There are many options to choose from. Here are a few examples:

  - DISC
  - Myers-Briggs
  - VIA Character Strengths
  - Strengths Finder

You're already special, with your own talents and strengths. Live your best life by making sure you're using them. Explore what makes you special using the ideas listed above and reflect on ways you can use your unique talents more.

_____

_____

_____

_____

_____

_____

_____

_____

_____

_____

_____

_____

_____

_____

_____

_____

_____

_____

_____

_____

_____

_____

# 14. The Power of Priming
*How your environment influences your thoughts*

A while back, I noticed that every time I sat down in my home office to work, I struggled to find any motivation. I would look at my to-do list and feel like I was in a fog. I shared my frustration with a dear friend who asked me what I thought the problem was. I said I wasn't sure, but I knew the piles of paper and clutter surrounding my desk weren't helping. She jumped on my comment immediately.

"Do you have a couple of empty boxes?" she asked. With boxes in hand, she proceeded to remove the messy contents on the horizontal surfaces. In less than 10 minutes, the office seemed larger, less oppressive, and I felt a sense of freedom. That initial shift fired up my motivation to sort through the boxes and the remaining clutter.

Then my friend informed me that she would help me create a space that was inviting, energizing, and that fueled my creativity. With her amazing skills, she redecorated my office into something I find truly inspiring. What a difference!

Why am I sharing this? My experience reminded me of a fascinating area of study called psychological priming. It shows how external factors influence our thinking and behavior without us even noticing. These influential factors include other people, physical surroundings, words, sounds, scents, temperature, colors, etc.[17] Studies have shown that excessive clutter can also play a role by overloading our senses, resulting in decreased performance and creativity, and increased stress.[18]

The exciting news is that we can take advantage of the power of priming because we have control over many aspects of our surroundings. Take a look around your living and work spaces. What could you change or eliminate that would create a more motivating and inspiring environment? If you're like me, you may benefit from asking a trusted friend for help.

_____

_____

_____

_____

_____

_____

_____

_____

_____

_____

_____

_____

_____

_____

_____

_____

_____

_____

_____

_____

_____

_____

_____

_____

## 15. Wouldn't It Be Great if Life Were Easy? Or Would It?
*Using PERMA to create your best life*

Wouldn't it be great if we could avoid all the struggles in our lives? If there were no challenges and everything always went the way we wanted? If our lives were easy and we had everything we needed all the time?

This idea sounds pretty nice—at least at first. But I've learned from my studies in Positive Psychology that these conditions would *not* create our best life. Just like we see in the lives of many of the rich and famous, we would get bored as the novelty wore off. We actually want challenges and get great satisfaction and self-confidence from overcoming obstacles.

Martin Seligman, considered the father of Positive Psychology, says there are five elements that can help people reach a life of lasting fulfillment, wellbeing, and meaning. He uses the acronym PERMA.[19]

- <u>Positive emotions</u>: These are emotions like happiness, curiosity, serenity, gratitude, pride, and hope. They make us feel good about ourselves and our world.

- <u>Engagement</u>: When we're engaged, we're entirely absorbed in the present moment, creating a flow of blissful immersion into the task or activity. This engaged flow is important for stretching our intelligence, skills, and emotional capabilities.

- <u>Relationships</u>: Relationships and social connections are one of the most important aspects of life because we are social animals. We thrive on connection, love, intimacy, and strong emotional and physical interactions with other people.

- <u>Meaning</u>: Meaning gives us a reason for our existence and a sense that there is a greater purpose to life. We realize everything is not just about us.

- Accomplishment: Having goals and overcoming challenges in life can give us a sense of achievement, pride, and fulfillment.

Reflect on each of these areas of PERMA and consider if any of them could use some improvement in your life. What actions can you take to build these personal elements?

_____

_____

_____

_____

_____

_____

_____

_____

_____

_____

_____

_____

_____

_____

_____

_____

_____

_____

_____

_____

_____

_____

## 16. Creative Gratitude:
*Why I'm grateful for singing in the shower, Star Trek and straws*

I know these sound like very strange things to be grateful for, but let me explain. My young daughter loves to belt out a song while showering. It warms my heart and makes me smile. It tells me she's happy and enjoying life, which makes me feel incredibly grateful.

*Star Trek*, both *The Next Generation* and *Voyager*, made the list because we had so much fun watching all the old episodes together as a family. We struggle to find shows everyone can enjoy, and episode usually had an interesting life lesson or philosophical question.

It may sound weird to be grateful for straws, but I have a genetic tremor that causes my hands to shake. It runs in my family. It can be an inconvenience, but it also makes me self-conscious when I'm trying to drink from a glass when I'm around other people. Tipping a full glass to my lips can take two hands, but a straw makes the task much easier.

I share these interesting examples as a reminder that we can get creative with gratitude. There are so many simple and everyday things that make our lives better. We can also think of people we wouldn't normally consider. For example, I'm very grateful for my daughter's bus driver and for his determination to get all the kids to school safely. How about appreciating a situation, an opportunity, or even something we don't have (see Tip 7)?

I challenge you to get creative with your gratitude and keep an eye out for unusual things you can be grateful for. We often limit ourselves to the common stuff like our health, our family, our home . . . These are important, but we could add a little fun by making a game out of it and looking for the uncommon. It also shifts our thinking because we're on the lookout for the good stuff around us.

What unusual things, people, places, and situations can you think of to be grateful for?

_____

_____

_____

_____

_____

_____

_____

_____

_____

_____

_____

_____

_____

_____

_____

_____

_____

_____

_____

_____

_____

_____

_____

# 17. You'll Want to Print This
## *A simple list for more positivity*

I have a confession: there are times when I forget to use the positivity tools in my toolbox. When I'm frustrated, upset, or feeling down, it can be hard to remember the many great strategies I know and share. I've learned this is normal, so I decided to make a list, print it out, and post it by my computer so I can't miss it. If you have a similar challenge, consider printing this list or making your own.

- Take 5-8 slow, deep breaths.

- Do something kind for someone else (maybe an email telling someone what you appreciate about them).

- Do some fun exercise/movement/dance.

- Listen to a favorite song. (Have a list you can choose from.)

- Spend some time with friends or family in-person, on the phone or using social media.

- Spend time with your pet.

- Get outside.

- Reread your favorite quotes.

- Think of good things that have happened in the past day or two.

- Watch a funny video or look at funny pictures. (They're easy to find on the internet.)

- Be grateful for the simple things in life that weren't available 20 years ago, 100 years ago, etc. (Like antibiotics, eyeglasses, microwaves, the internet, indoor plumbing—you get the idea.)

- Be grateful for a particular person in your life and think about why.

- Be grateful for situations and opportunities in your life.

- Read or reread a book that inspires you.

- Think of a memory that lifts your spirits.

- Spend time remembering a past success.

- Smile and make sure you crinkle the corners of your eyes! See Tip 12.

Reflect on how you could use a few of these tips in the next week. Add other strategies you use or would like to try.

_____

_____

_____

_____

_____

_____

_____

_____

_____

_____

_____

_____

_____

_____

_____

_____

# 18. Don't Think About Gratitude—Feel It
*There's an important difference*

We hear a lot about the value of taking time for gratitude. Research shows it can help us sleep better, be more optimistic, more easily forgive others, improve our immune system, and more.[20]

Yet if we only *think* about gratitude, we miss out on most of the benefits. We can quickly come up with a list of things we're grateful for without experiencing a connection to them. But if we want to truly *feel* grateful, it needs to be heartfelt and more than just a thought. It's funny how I can notice the difference. If I just *think* of something I appreciate, I don't feel any different. But when I *feel* grateful, there is an emotional and physical shift. Studies show that this is caused by chemical changes in our body that improve our physical and emotional wellbeing.[21]

How can we move beyond thinking about gratitude to feeling it? Various approaches will work differently for each of us, but here are some of my favorite strategies you can try:

- Have a discussion with someone else. Share what you're grateful for and provide background and context to the other person. Talking can help bring it to life.

- Reflect on *why* you're grateful for something or someone. Why is it helpful or beneficial for you or your life? Keep digging to find the true "Why."

- Consider how your life would be without this thing or person. The trick is to do this without taking it to the point that you feel sad about the possibility of losing it or them—just enough to really feel appreciation.

- Create a mood or environment that makes it easier to feel the emotion of gratitude. Maybe it starts with listening to a favorite song that touches your heart or remembering a special time that helps you feel heart-centered.

Give one or two of these a try and reflect on the difference between just thinking vs. feeling gratitude. Things you might choose to appreciate could include a person, a place, a situation, a thing, an opportunity, or even something you're glad you *don't* have. You could find things from your current life, your past, or even things you're looking forward to. See Tips 5, 7, and 16.

_____

_____

_____

_____

_____

_____

_____

_____

_____

_____

_____

_____

_____

_____

_____

_____

_____

_____

_____

_____

_____

# 19. Amplify the Power of Your Thoughts
*Change your posture to change your mind*

I'm fascinated by how our thoughts affect our mood and our reality. But there's also an emerging area of intriguing research that shows how our body posture influences our minds. Just think about it. You're feeling worried about an upcoming project, or maybe even worried about your job. It's draining your energy and motivation, which will hurt your ability to give the project your best. Your body language may become slouched and hunched, sending signals to your brain that you're powerless and helpless, which reinforces your worry. Just shifting your body posture to a more expansive and powerful pose changes the messages to your brain and influences what you believe.[22]

The body and the brain share a two-way communication—they each affect the other in ways that don't always seem obvious. For example, research suggests that your arms, your facial expressions, and even your hand gestures influence your mind, mood, and behavior.[23] What if you could capture valuable synergy by using both of these approaches together? While you're holding an upright, open pose, you could remember a past success, a time when you felt proud of an achievement, or you could think of things you're grateful for in your work or life. I've found that it's harder to feel grateful when I'm hunched over or to feel confident in my abilities when I'm slouching versus when I'm standing with my arms raised to the sky. Try it for yourself. Sit huddled in a chair and think of a happy memory. Now, remember the same memory while standing with your feet apart and your hands on your hips or over your head. Which leaves you with more positive energy?

I love how social psychologist Amy Cuddy expresses this phenomenon, "The way you carry yourself is a source of personal power—the kind of power that is the key to presence. It's the key that allows you to unlock yourself—your abilities, your creativity, your courage, and even your generosity. It doesn't give you skills or talents you don't have; it helps you to share the ones you do have. It doesn't make you smarter or better informed; it makes you more resilient and open. It doesn't change who you are; it allows you to *be* who you are."[24]

Reflect on how you can use your posture to enhance your personal positivity. What are some examples or situations where this would be useful?

_____

_____

_____

_____

_____

_____

_____

_____

_____

_____

_____

_____

_____

_____

_____

_____

_____

_____

## 20. Every Situation Is an Opportunity
*Practice makes perfect*

Have you ever read a book that describes how to learn something new like driving a car or playing the guitar? When you finished the book, were you ready to navigate the highways of New York City or play onstage in a band?

Information and knowledge are useful and necessary for us to learn and grow, but they're often only part of the equation. The real learning takes place when we're practicing behind the wheel of the car or with the guitar in our hands. Even then, it takes hours and hours of practice before we're ready to take on bigger challenges like heavy traffic or performing for a live audience.

The same phenomenon applies to training our minds to notice more of the positive all around us. Just reading and hearing about how to be happier and more positive doesn't make us so. We need situations in our lives where we can *apply* the information we've learned so we can get better at choosing our thoughts and actions.

Life is great at providing us with many opportunities to practice. If we can see these challenges in a new light, we can use them to build our resilience and get better at managing our stress. Whether it's getting rear-ended, losing our cell phone, or spilling coffee on our clothes, these situations offer opportunities for choosing our response. And when we practice applying what we've learned to the little, easy challenges, we're preparing ourselves to handle those larger, more difficult situations that life is bound to throw at us.

What opportunities to practice choosing your thoughts and actions has life provided for you recently? Were you able to apply your tools? What could you have done differently?

Now we have a reason to be thankful for those little annoyances in our lives!

# 21. Let's Get Laughing
*It really is great medicine*

Have you laughed out loud today? You should! More and more research shows that laughing is so good for us physically and mentally.[25] It's a powerful antidote to stress, pain, and conflict. Check out these benefits of laughter:

- Relieves physical tension and stress
- Boosts the immune system
- Triggers the release of endorphins, the body's natural feel-good chemicals
- Benefits heart health
- Counteracts distressing emotions
- Increases energy

Yet many of us—including myself—laugh less often and more quietly once we become adults. My young daughter has no problem giggling uncontrollably. I have much to learn from her. I'm working on laughing more easily and louder—and not being embarrassed by it.

I look for reasons to laugh. Sometimes it's a funny animal video on YouTube™. Sometimes it's even a smart comment my husband makes or one of my daughter's funny faces. Laughing is contagious, so being around others who laugh easily is helpful. Watching stand-up comedy might be an option for you. Laughter yoga and laughter clubs are gaining popularity and are great fun, too.

I remember my first laughter yoga experience. I'm a little shy and reserved, so I wasn't sure if I'd like it. The teacher told us we would fake our laughter at first, but it would become real as we got into it. Sure enough, as I tried to chortle and chuckle, I started to really giggle listening to the ridiculous howls and snorts of my classmates. Pretty soon I found myself laughing real belly laughs that were hard to stop. At the end of class, I felt energized and relaxed at the same time.

With today's technology and all of our devices, it's easier than ever to find things that will tickle our funny bone. What are some things you could do to add more laughter to your day?

_____

_____

_____

_____

_____

_____

_____

_____

_____

_____

_____

_____

_____

_____

_____

_____

_____

_____

_____

_____

_____

_____

# 22. Can Chores Make Us Happier?
*Try adding some mindfulness*

If you're like me, you probably hurry to finish a chore so you can rush to get the next chore done. What if instead, we chose to be mindful and to savor the task? I was busy folding clothes the other day—wanting to finish quickly so I could get to the next to-do on my list. Then I remembered a mindfulness article I'd recently read. Mindfulness is about having a purposeful awareness of the present moment to help focus our constantly wandering minds. I decided to take this opportunity to practice.

I became aware of the smell of the fresh laundry and the feel of the clothes in my hands. Then I thought about how grateful I was to be healthy enough to do my own laundry and to have the ability to do it in my home instead of hauling it all to a laundromat. I noticed that I was folding clothes for my daughter and husband, which reminded me of how fortunate I am to have them in my life. A common, thoughtless chore suddenly became a positive experience that lightened my mood and made my day a little brighter.

It reminds me of a quote I read online—"The things you take for granted, someone else is praying for." —Author Unknown

I now try to apply this approach to other chores. I love mowing the lawn on a warm, sunny day, smelling the aroma of fresh cut grass. I also enjoy the ability to zone out as I slowly drive the riding mower around the yard. I find that cooking can be calming when I take a mindful approach, focusing on each ingredient and step in the recipe.

What everyday tasks can you use as a mood-boosting opportunity?

# 23. Struggling to Finish
### *The difference a little encouragement can make*

I'll never forget the first time I ran an actual 5K (3.1 mile) race. I've never been much of a runner, but I had a few friends who were doing the race, so I thought I would give it a try. The first mile wasn't bad, but the second mile started to get harder. By the time I was into the third mile, I was tired and in pain. I had a side stitch and knew I was going to have to stop before the finish line.

Then I came around a corner and noticed some people on the side of the street. As they saw me coming, they started hollering and cheering. A couple people even had signs that read "You can do it!" How amazing! These people that I'd never met were yelling for and encouraging *me*! I felt a rush of energy. Their words and enthusiasm fueled me so I could keep going. It was a fantastic experience!

What if we encouraged and cheered each other on more in our daily lives? How might it fuel and motivate us to keep going, especially when things seem overwhelming or hard? I have a few dear friends who have shown me how good this can feel. What a gift when I'm feeling discouraged, doubting my abilities, or feeling overwhelmed! The wonderful thing is, it brings me great joy to encourage and support them, too.

Who do you know that could use a little extra encouragement? Consider emailing or calling them to show your support. Or consider reaching out to an understanding friend if *you* could use a little motivation yourself. You never know how big of an impact it can have on them—*and* on you.

## 24. Using Your Imagination
*Creating a best-case scenario*

When we were kids, we had great imaginations. We could envision dragons, monsters, and castles with kings and queens. We could imagine that we had superpowers and were battling the bad guys to save the world. We might have visited magical lands and made trips to outer space. Then somewhere along the line, as we grew older, our imaginations changed.

Some say we lose our imaginations as adults, but actually they're still very powerful. It's just that now, we tend to imagine worst-case scenarios and all the things that could go wrong. In fact, our imaginations are so vivid that we can get ourselves worked up with anxiety, frustration, or anger about something that's never even happened. For example, when winter approaches, I can become stressed when I imagine getting stuck in the snow and missing a meeting or talk I'm scheduled to give.

What if we *also* imagined the best possibilities, such as a great future with amazing success? What if we imagined the world was out to do us good and that everyone had the best of intentions? How might this change the way we approached our day? I try to remember to use this strategy in my business. When I have an upcoming presentation, I intentionally imagine everything going great. I envision having fun and connecting with the audience. I imagine my message having a huge impact on people's lives, and many people benefiting from what I share. Which approach do you think gives me more confidence and enthusiasm?

This can be a great practice to do at bedtime or first thing in the morning. Just take a few moments and imagine wonderful things happening in your life. What do you see?

# 25. Can Passwords Boost Your Mood?
*Using letters and numbers to brighten your day*

H ere's a riddle. What do we keep forgetting and don't want, but without them, we can forget about getting what we want?

Of course, the answer is *passwords*! Those ever-annoying, necessary but pesky combinations of letters and numbers we're constantly typing into our computers and devices. What if every time we typed one in, it brought a favorite song to our lips, a special memory to our minds, a warm love to our hearts, or an optimistic spin to our attitude? It's possible if we use *positive* passwords.

It's easy to let our minds instinctively focus on all the things we don't like about our job, co-workers, or boss. We can get sucked into the politics, the drama, the overwhelm, and the emergency fires. What better place to use a reminder that we can *choose* what we focus on. For example, we could create a password, **Tictntg4&** that stands for "Today I choose to notice the good" with a number and symbol if your system requires the extra security. Another possibility might be **Img4ml***—"I am grateful for my life." The best approach is to customize it for your situation.

Other great options include using your password to remind you of a favorite song. How about **IMalright** for "I'm Alright" by Kenny Loggins? Or **B!domlife** for "Best Day of My Life" by American Authors? Another one of my favorites is "September" by Earth, Wind, & Fire, which could be **DinSept33** for "Dancing in September." Again, you can always add numbers or symbols if your system requires. Don't you feel better when you have a good song going through your head? Which songs lift your spirits?

How about creating a password that reminds you of a wonderful memory, favorite movie scene, or your pet? You could use it to remind you of an intention or goal.

In every moment we have the choice to create our own experience by what we focus on and how we respond. Using passwords to shift us towards the positive is a great place to start! What are some positive passwords ideas you could use?

_____

_____

_____

_____

_____

_____

_____

_____

_____

_____

_____

_____

_____

_____

_____

_____

_____

_____

_____

_____

_____

_____

# 26. Personalized Positivity
*Experimenting to find what works for you*

I find it exciting that we live in a time where advances in science have led to understanding the need for personalized medicine—because we're all different.[26] We're even seeing initial findings in the study of nutrition that have led to understanding the need for a personalized healthy diet—because we're all different.[27] And advances in Positive Psychology have led to understanding the need for personalized strategies for greater happiness and positivity—because we're all different.[28]

Since my background is in science, I like to tell people that we all need to *experiment* with the different approaches from Positive Psychology and find what works for us. My favorite practice might not be a good fit for someone else. The gratitude journaling your best friend loves might not work for you. The visualization exercise that's made such a difference for you might do nothing for your partner.

After learning and trying many different practices, I've found that three of my favorite daily go-to "exercises" are:

- Taking several slow, deep breaths when I'm feeling anxious (check out Tip 40)

- Smiling with my eyes to boost my mood (learn more in Tip 12)

- Sharing three good things from my day with friends or family to get better at noticing the good

There are many factors that can affect how well something resonates with us, like our personality, our lifestyle, our values, our past, etc. Studies show that we need to pick a strategy and then try it for a week or two to see if we like it. If it's rewarding, fun, or impactful, it's easier to keep going. If we stick with it and repeat it often, we can actually create new connections in our brains that have a lasting impact on our ability to be more positive, and ultimately, on our quality of life.

Take a look at some of the ideas listed in Tip 17 to choose from and experiment with this week. Write about your experiences with them below.

_____

_____

_____

_____

_____

_____

_____

_____

_____

_____

_____

_____

_____

_____

_____

_____

_____

_____

_____

## 27. Don't Wait for Happiness
*Remembering to enjoy the present moment*

Do you remember, as a teenager, being so excited about getting your driver's license and eventually, your own set of wheels? I bet when it finally happened, you were thrilled! At some point, did that thrill wear off? Maybe your mom wanted you to drive to the grocery store and run errands. Maybe you had to pay for the car or insurance. Maybe your friends wanted you to taxi them everywhere.

I remember living in an apartment thinking how happy I'd be once I had my own house without neighbors above and below me making noise. When my husband and I *did* move into our own house, I wished there was less traffic on our road and that we didn't live around so many other houses. Then we moved into our dream place out in the country. It's perfect! But I often forget to appreciate all the things I waited so long to have.

There are major events in our lives that we expect will bring us great happiness—like getting a job, receiving a promotion, buying a house, getting married, starting a family, etc. These do make us happier—for a while. However, once we experience them, the novelty eventually wears off, and we may think we need to wait for the next big event to find happiness again. "I can't wait until the kids leave home. Then I'll be happy." Or, "Once I retire, then I'll be happy!" Scientists call this hedonic adaptation.

Being excited and looking forward to an upcoming event *is* a good thing. But the catch is, we shouldn't rely on the future for our wellbeing and happiness. We should anticipate and savor life's big occasions, but we should *also* enjoy the journey and the time in between.

So, don't wait to be happy! Practice choosing a mindset that reminds you of all the wonderful things around you *now* and of all that you have to be grateful for *today* so you can appreciate and be happy in the present moment.

Can you think of times in your life when you were anticipating something that you thought would make you happy? Is there something that you're waiting for now to make you happier?

_____

_____

_____

_____

_____

_____

_____

_____

_____

_____

_____

_____

_____

_____

_____

_____

_____

_____

_____

_____

_____

# 28. It's Better to Give than Receive
*The power of social support*

We've all probably heard the adage that it's better to give than receive. But this isn't just a saying, there's actual research that shows *this is true* for our success and wellbeing.[29, 30] The "giving" I'm referring to is social support.

When we are there for our friends, supportive of our family, and encouraging to coworkers, *we* are actually better off. Research shows we're more engaged and satisfied with our jobs and that leads to more success at work. Giving this support also has many health benefits including reducing our stress, lowering our blood pressure, and even helping us live longer.

As with most things in life, we need a healthy balance. It's important to be careful to also consider our own time and energy and not overdo it. For example, these benefits don't necessarily hold true for caregivers, who end up with lower wellbeing and higher risk for depression.

Looking at these studies made me reflect on examples in my own life. I greatly appreciate offers of help and encouragement from my family and friends, but I also feel really good when I get the opportunity to *give to others*. It's so fun to help my friends remember and celebrate their progress and achievements. When someone is feeling discouraged, I find it very rewarding to help them shift to see how far they've come and how much they've learned. It's very fulfilling when I can share something I've learned to help someone else.

It reminds me of the quote by author and speaker Zig Ziglar, "You can have everything in life you want if you will just help other people get what they want."

In what ways have you supported and encouraged others lately? Try experimenting with offering more social support to others and see how you feel. What are some examples you could try?

# Section 2:

## MANAGING
# NEGATIVITY

## 29. Why I Love My Kitchen Sink
*Using inconvenience as an opportunity for gratitude*

Our kitchen faucet had developed a leak. Every time I turned it on, little sprays from pinholes in the faucet would give me a shower. It was toast! This was going to be a terrible inconvenience! Without my faucet, I couldn't easily wash produce, rinse dishes, wash my hands, wipe counters, etc.

I rushed to the hardware store to buy a new faucet, but when I brought it home, it didn't fit. More frustration! By now, my husband and I should realize that when it comes to plumbing projects, we need to multiply the time we *think* it's going to require to fix it by a factor of 20—or more. Things never go as smoothly as anticipated, and it usually takes multiple trips to the store.

My instinct was to feel irritated and impatient to get it fixed. Was there another way to look at this inconvenience?

Instead, I tried to shift my perspective and realize that I should appreciate how wonderful it is to have hot and cold running water in the kitchen. It wasn't so many generations ago that it wasn't that common. I remember hearing stories of my grandparents heating up water on the stove for dishes and baths. It also reminded me that many people around the world will live their entire lives without ever enjoying indoor plumbing or a faucet with hot water.

Another thing I was grateful for was that my husband was able to install the new faucet so we didn't have to hire a plumber. And despite the challenges, I only had to suffer through *one* day without a working faucet in the kitchen.

The sink is now fully functional, and I often try to pause and enjoy having running water in my kitchen. What a great gift!

Reflect on a recent inconvenience or unwanted situation that made you frustrated. Is there a way to take a different view and use it to remind yourself of something positive?

_____

_____

_____

_____

_____

_____

_____

_____

_____

_____

_____

_____

_____

_____

_____

_____

_____

_____

_____

_____

_____

_____

_____

# 30. Don't Let 'Ants' Get the Better of You
*Squashing Automatic Negative Thoughts (ANTS)*

I love this acronym! ANTS are Automatic Negative Thoughts.

For example:

- *You never listen to me.*
- *They don't like me.*
- *This situation is not going to work out. I know something bad will happen.*

ANTS cause us to look at the future with anxiety and pessimism. What if. . .? They cause us to regret our past and be unsatisfied with the present. ANTS cause chemical changes in our brains and bodies that make us feel bad and behave in ways that distance us from others. Consider this—if you aren't *thinking* about your thoughts (how often does this happen?), they're automatic and are not necessarily true. But, because we think them, we assume they must be true. This includes thoughts about ourselves, others, our world, our work, etc.

**Eliminating Ants**

What I love about ANTS is that we can do something about them. Physician, psychiatrist, and author Daniel Amen recommends these three steps.[31]

- Write them down to gain clarity.

- Ask yourself if these thoughts are true.

- Talk back. Consider why they might *not* be true or *what else* is true. If you struggle with this part, it can be useful to recruit a trusted friend or family member to help you gain perspective.

Here are a couple of my favorite examples:

**ANT:**    My boss doesn't like me.

**Response:** I don't know that. Maybe she's just having a bad day. Bosses are people, too.

**ANT:**    I'm stupid.

**Response:** Sometimes I do things that aren't too smart, but I'm not stupid.

**ANT:**    I'll never be a success like _____ (fill in the blank)

**Response:** We all have different talents and strengths. I may have different ones than _____ and I may need to learn the best ways to apply them.

Give it a try! See if you can identify and squash a few of your ANTS.

_____

_____

_____

_____

_____

_____

_____

_____

_____

_____

_____

_____

_____

# 31. I'm Mad All Over Again!
*Reliving past negative situations*

The day we brought our newborn daughter home from the hospital was amazingly special *and* amazingly frustrating! Frustrating because when we got home, we discovered that the contractor we'd hired had decided to start remodeling our basement while we were at the hospital. What we saw made us incredibly mad and disappointed! We discovered that they had cut the windows in the basement concrete wall larger, as we had requested, but the cuts were terribly crooked, the window holes were the wrong size, and they had "accidentally" cut the sill plate, the important foundation that the rest of the house is built upon.

When we called the contractor, he told us these were not important issues and not to worry about them—he would cover everything up so we would never notice. As we emphasized our dissatisfaction and pushed to have them fixed instead of covered up, he finally admitted he and his crew had been hung-over when they'd worked on our house. He then proceeded to tell us that if we wanted him to do this "extra" work, we would have to pay more. As you can imagine, we were furious!

All of this happened almost 11 years ago, but just writing these words brings up a lot of anger and negative energy. I can feel my chest tighten and my teeth clench. Even now, when I see an ad or truck with the contractor's company name, I can feel a strong wave of frustration hit me.

I now realize that this "replaying" is totally normal. It's a survival mechanism wired into our brains to help keep us safe and avoid future harm. I've also learned that it's easy to get caught up in these past negative memories and relive all of the associated emotions. The trick is to *notice* our thoughts and realize *we can change them*. We can distract ourselves (see Tip 38), or we can choose to focus on something we're grateful for (see Tips 5, 7, and 16).

Think of a past situation that brings back a surge of negative emotions. Reflect on how you could tune in, thank your brain for keeping you safe, and avoid getting stuck by intentionally choosing to shift your thoughts. It gets easier with practice.

# 32. Don't Be so Hard on Yourself
*No experience is wasted*

Have you ever made a decision that you later regretted? Maybe it was a job you took (I have a couple of those!), a group you joined, or an expensive item you purchased. In fact, maybe you're stressing over a choice you have right now. I've seen this with young friends who are feeling the pressure to decide what college to attend or what major to choose. Which is the right choice and which is the wrong one for their best future? Nobody wants to waste a bunch of time traveling down the wrong path.

Here's another way to look at it.

**Past Decisions**

You can't change past decisions. For whatever reason, it probably seemed like the right thing to do at the time. However, you can change the way you think about it. Instead of feeling regret or remorse, shift your perspective and realize that your choice gave you some important things:

- **Experience:** You gained new skills, wisdom, and insights about yourself and the world to help you with future choices.

- **Connections:** You likely met new people with new ideas, and you had an influence on people you encountered along the way.

- **Growth:** You grew as a person, building character and resilience, so you're better prepared for future challenges.

**Current Decisions**

Don't get too stressed about a current decision. If the choice is difficult, chances are they're all good options. We often think one choice must be better than another, but many times we put unnecessary pressure on ourselves. Even if we later think we should have made a different choice, we can remind ourselves that we will learn, grow, and gain new connections from our current path. No experience is wasted.

In the past few months, I've had a couple of conversations with people lamenting past mistakes they've felt they made with their lives. I pointed out that those "mistakes" have helped them learn how to make better choices and have shaped their thinking and the opportunities and possibilities they now see.

What past choices do you regret that have actually been important stepping-stones that led you to where you needed to be?

_____

_____

_____

_____

_____

_____

_____

_____

_____

_____

_____

_____

_____

_____

_____

_____

# 33. Don't Put on a Happy Face
## *Negative emotions serve a purpose*

I've noticed a theme over these past few months. Several people have told me that they've been trying to be positive and upbeat, but it's been very difficult lately. After talking more, it turns out they were feeling sad about a loss. In some cases it was a loss of health, a job, or a loved one. They didn't want to burden others, so they tried to hide it. I suggested that they give themselves permission to be sad.

A common misconception about increasing our positivity is that we aren't supposed to feel bad, and we certainly shouldn't let others know we're feeling sad, frustrated, or worried. But negative emotions are totally normal, *and* they serve a purpose. Without them, we would not have survived as a species (see Tip 37).

In his article *Beyond Happiness: The Upside of Feeling Down,* Matthew Hutson comments, "Negative emotions do us a great favor: They save us from ourselves. They're signals urging us to change what we're doing—and they're actually necessary for feeling good." Research indicates that accepting negative feelings such as sadness can lower depression. It helps us avoid the extra burden of feeling bad for feeling bad.[32]

Hutson points out, "Sadness also functions as a signal to others that we may need help." When we share our real feelings with others, it reveals our humanity and can help us connect more deeply with others. We also give them permission to share *their* true emotions.

Some keys to working with negative emotions:

• Don't avoid or suppress them. Acknowledge how you feel.

• Look for the information they're trying to tell you. For example, is there an action you need to take?

- Don't get stuck there. Distract yourself if you start going into a downward spiral.

- Avoid unnecessary negativity, such as replaying a past situation that makes you upset without any benefit to you (see Tip 48) or worrying about things outside your control.

Can you think of a time when you felt a negative emotion like sadness, anger, or anxiety? Did you carefully acknowledge and express it or did you suppress it? Is there anything you could've done differently based on the points above?

_____

_____

_____

_____

_____

_____

_____

_____

_____

_____

_____

_____

_____

_____

_____

_____

## 34. Trauma Can Lead to Growth
*The flip side of PTSD*

Most people are familiar with the term post-traumatic stress disorder or PTSD—the condition that can occur after someone experiences or witnesses a traumatic event. The result can be unexplained stress and fear that make it difficult for someone to function normally in their everyday life. What may surprise you is that people who have a traumatic event in their lives are more likely to experience post-traumatic *growth* or PTG.[33] These people discover a renewed appreciation for life, finding it easier and more enjoyable than before. Yet few people have ever heard of this term.

The data shows that there are often three ways in which people's lives improve:[34]

- **Improved relationships:** For example, they may value their friends and family more and feel an increased sense of compassion for others.

- **Seeing themselves differently:** For example, they may feel they have personal strength and resilience while accepting their weaknesses and limitations.

- **Changing their life philosophy:** For example, they may feel appreciation for each new day with a better ability to live in the present and re-evaluate their priorities and values in life.

Just to be clear, this does *not* mean that these people bypass the suffering and pain before finding a different path. It does mean that they don't get *stuck* there. They overcome the downward spiral and find a way to grow and learn. In one study on women with breast cancer, pessimists were as likely to experience PTG as optimists. Another study shows that those who felt more depressed after their diagnoses were more likely to say they had made positive changes up to two years later, compared with those who found the ordeal less trying. Some reported that their newfound strength came from thinking, "If I can get through this, I can get through anything."[35] Why is knowing about post-traumatic growth important? There's a theory that if more people were aware of this possibility, more people would have the hope needed to rise above their fear and anxiety after a traumatic event. Statistically, there's a good chance that all of us will have a traumatic experience in our lives, so let's be prepared.

Have you had a traumatic event in your life? Reflect on how it's changed you, or envision a possible future trauma and how this information could provide hope.

_____

_____

_____

_____

_____

_____

_____

_____

_____

_____

_____

_____

_____

_____

_____

_____

_____

# 35. When You're in a Funk
## *How to get back up when you're down*

You know the feeling. You're down, and you don't want to feel better. You're not interested in doing anything, especially anything fun or positive. You have no interest in listening to an upbeat song much less watching a funny video. Maybe something triggered it. Maybe a few things happened that were disappointing, frustrating, or sad that culminated into your overall sense of melancholy. Or maybe nothing happened—this feeling just crept over you, and now you can't shake it.

I'm not talking about depression—a serious down feeling that hangs on for many days or longer, affects the quality of your life, and should be treated by a professional. The funk I'm talking about is unusual or at least doesn't happen very often. It saps your enjoyment of life. Nothing seems worthwhile, so why bother. Maybe you even feel like a failure or a fraud.

Here are some ideas of how to dispel the funk:

- Call an understanding friend that you can share your feelings with.

- Think of something nice you can do for someone else. It may just be emailing them a note. It helps to get the focus off your own life.

- Distract yourself with a movie or book.

- If you can muster the motivation, get outside and go for a walk.

- Just wait for it to pass. Realize it won't last, and more than likely you'll feel better in the morning.

- Give yourself permission to feel down, but set a time limit.

It can be very helpful to share how you're feeling with those around you. Just saying, "I'm having a down day" or "I'm sorry if I'm acting strange, but I'm just in a funk today" is very helpful. Then, they're not wondering what they did wrong to make you mad or telling themselves stories to try to explain your behavior.

What do you do when you're in a funk? What could you do? Keep your list handy for the day you might need it.

_____

_____

_____

_____

_____

_____

_____

_____

_____

_____

_____

_____

_____

_____

_____

_____

_____

_____

_____

_____

# 36. Now Is Not the Time to Give Up
## *Letting your discouragement pass*

Think back to a time when you were frustrated because something you were working on wasn't going well. Maybe it was something small like trying to figure out a new app or program on your device that seemed easy at first. Or maybe it was a big project or goal you'd been working on for a long time, and you were almost done. Suddenly, you hit a serious roadblock. Did you feel hopelessness or anger? Did you feel like giving up?

This is *not* the time to decide to throw in the towel! Here's something important I've learned—when we feel this frustrated, our emotions overtake our logical thinking. Studies show that we become so focused on the problem, we can't step back to see other possible approaches. This is because of biochemical and physiological changes that interfere with our ability to think clearly in these moments. The best thing we can do is to take a break and walk away. We need to distract ourselves and allow time for our body and brain to regain balance so we can think rationally (see Tip 38).

My husband's work seems to give him a constant supply of experiences to practice this approach. He owns a machine shop and does a variety of custom jobs. The other day, he had a job that included a part whose final geometry and finish were especially challenging. A few days into it, he told me he was done for the day because he'd hit a roadblock. His approach wasn't working, and he was stuck! His frustration was very high, and I could tell he was wondering if he would ever be able to finish this project. But after several hours of focusing on something else, he suddenly exclaimed that he'd figured out how to do it. I was very impressed and proud of his perseverance!

Can you remember a time when you were upset because of a setback and wanted to give up? What did you do? What could you have done differently?

# 37. Can It Be Good to Feel Bad?
## *The benefits of negative emotions*

I talk a lot about focusing on the good, but research shows there are times it can be helpful to focus on the bad. While feeling good helps us think more broadly and consider more ideas, negative emotions focus our minds on the problem.[36] They kick us into survival mode, providing us with anxiety and stress hormones that can give us the energy to deal with obstacles. The trick is to not get so overwhelmed by anxiety that it immobilizes us. This is where several deep breaths can be a big help (see Tip 40). Let's say you suddenly realize you only have two days to finish that big project and a wave of stress washes over you. That strong feeling of urgency can help you focus on finishing the project and give you the determination to get it done.

Feeling bad or upset can also be a signal that something is wrong.[37] Getting to the cause of the feelings can help us decide if we need to take action or make a change. The stress from realizing your project deadline is coming up fast is a signal that you need to do something. Another signal could be feeling upset because you think your partner doesn't appreciate you. Instead of feeling angry, it may be time to have a heart-to-heart talk with them to help them understand your needs. Or it could be simply shifting your focus to the things they do to show their appreciation—like making you dinner (see Tip 62).

Another example of when a negative emotion can be the better choice is when the risk is high, and it's better to be cautious instead of overly optimistic. For example, it may be safer to be *concerned* that the roads are too icy to go shopping or that the campfire hasn't died down enough to go to bed instead of being overly optimistic that everything is fine. It may be good to be *worried* that your family doesn't know where you are, and you feel it's important to give them a call. We need to pay attention to that negative nagging doubt and anxiety.

Can you think of a time when you were feeling anxious or angry? Consider what information your emotion was trying to tell you. Did you listen? What could you do differently next time?

_____

_____

_____

_____

_____

_____

_____

_____

_____

_____

_____

_____

_____

_____

_____

_____

_____

_____

_____

_____

_____

_____

# 38. Help! I Need a Distraction
## *When stressful emotions cause you to lose perspective*

When we're immersed in stress or anxiety, our bodies undergo a chemical change that affects our ability to think rationally. One of these changes is the release of the stress hormone cortisol. Cortisol prepares us for an emergency by triggering the fight-or-flight response. But it also causes us to lose perspective and makes us more sensitive to other minor stressors that can result in a downward spiral. Sound familiar?

It's helpful to remember that we might not want to make important decisions when we're really frustrated or upset. It also means that it may not be easy to reason with someone else who is struggling with their own stressful emotions.

I had the opportunity to experience this firsthand when I was playing Monopoly with my daughter, who was nine at the time. Luck was on my side, and I couldn't do anything wrong. Everything I touched turned to money. My daughter, on the other hand, was having the worst luck ever. She was trying to hold it together, but it was obvious she was struggling. When she finally lost, she could no longer control her frustration. She cried and said she wanted to throw and break things. I knew her body was swimming in cortisol, and she could only focus on her irritation. There was no chance of reasoning with her that it was just a game. I tried to listen and validate her feelings. I reminded her that it's OK to feel upset and vocalize our strong emotions, but we still need to control what we say and do, because destructive behavior and insults are *not* OK.

These kinds of stressful emotions are *not* fun. Yet I reminded myself that this was good practice for my daughter to learn how to deal with them. I was also having my own lessons in resisting being triggered by her strong emotions. I knew she needed time for her body to chemically reset, so I suggested that she distract herself by watching a video. Ta-da! In 15 minutes, she was back to her normal self. Phew!

Stressful emotions can be helpful by providing important information (see Tip 37). But the trick is not to get stuck and let them spiral out of control. Here is where finding a short-term distraction can be very helpful to take our minds off our problems and let the cortisol purge from our systems. Distractions such as watching a video, reading a book, listening to an upbeat song or exercise can be just the ticket.

What kinds of distractions help you when you're feeling upset or stressed? Which types of distractions could you try in the future?

_____

_____

_____

_____

_____

_____

_____

_____

_____

_____

_____

_____

_____

_____

_____

# 39. Watch Out for This 'Friend'
## *Tuning into your internal voice*

You may not realize it, but there's a good chance you have a friend that's bringing you down. Let's say you get passed over for a job or promotion. You likely have a friend who tells you that you don't deserve it—that you aren't talented enough or smart enough. They even keep reminding you of this rejection. Or perhaps you're trying to lose weight, but just can't manage to keep it off or get to your desired weight. Your "bad" friend tells you that you don't have enough willpower or that you're too weak and don't try hard enough. Or maybe you mess up on the job just enough to get your boss's attention and a small reprimand. Your friend reminds you of this over and over. They tell you that you never do things right and you aren't good enough to have this job.

I'm guessing right now that you're thinking you would never keep such a negative person as a friend. But the person I'm referring to in the above examples is not someone you can ignore or avoid. It's your own internal voice. These stories or messages are things many of us tell ourselves. If we could somehow make our thoughts a separate person, it's quite likely we wouldn't want to spend much time with them.

What can we do? We can tune in and be aware of our internal voice. If we notice it's stuck in a negative thought that's not doing us any good, we can purposely choose to focus on something more positive or change the story we're telling ourselves (see Tips 30 and 47). It may not be easy at first, but it does get easier with practice as we become a better friend to ourselves.

Can you think of a situation where you were not a good friend to yourself? What did you tell yourself? What could you do differently?

# 40. Help from Healing Breaths
*Shifting out of reactive mode*

I remember the first time I heard Rick Hanson talk about our bodies' re-active mode and how I found it extremely helpful. Hanson, a psychologist, Senior Fellow at the Greater Good Science Center at UC-Berkeley, and author, says we can think of our brains and bodies as having two modes of operation.[38] The first is "responsive mode," where our resources and energy are used to help our bodies heal, revitalize, re-energize, and basically take good care of ourselves. In responsive mode, we tend to be in a good mood and experience positive feelings.

The other setting, "reactive mode," is when our bodies are anticipating an emergency. Now our resources and energy are diverted to prepare us for fight-or-flight. Our brains have signaled that something is wrong, and we need to get ready to take action. Our heart rate increases. Our blood pressure rises along with our cortisol and adrenaline levels. Our pupils dilate and our muscles tense. Our mood is usually not good, and we're more likely to feel emotions such as anxiety, anger, and frustration.

Reactive mode is perfect if we really do need to fight for our lives or run out of a burning building. But if this mode is constantly being triggered by everyday stresses in our lives, our physical health can suffer. Our bodies aren't able to heal and rejuvenate as needed. Some experts believe that if we don't spend enough time in responsive mode, it can promote heart disease, immune disorders, and even cancer.[39]

A helpful practice I use is to notice when I'm feeling unnecessarily stressed and to think *healing breath* as I inhale and exhale deeply and slowly. I do this several times in a row. Taking slow breaths is a great way to activate our parasympathetic nervous system, which lowers our heart rate and blood pressure so we can shift back into responsive mode.

Can you think of a time when you were stressed? How could a few healing breaths have made it better? Think of future situations where you could use this practice.

_____

_____

_____

_____

_____

_____

_____

_____

_____

_____

_____

_____

_____

_____

_____

_____

_____

_____

_____

_____

_____

# 41. What Do You 'Get' to Do?
## *The power of switching one word*

It's a Monday morning, so I have to wake up extra early because I have to help my daughter get ready for school. I have to pack her a lunch and a snack, and then I have to do some laundry—the clothes are piling up! Next on my list, I have to work on an article for my business, and then I have to start prepping for a talk I have in a few days. There are some emails and calls I have to return. Phew! So much I have to do!

Reading this makes me feel overwhelmed and exhausted.

**Going from 'have to' to 'get to'**
Watch what happens when I make a simple switch with the word "have" to "get."

It's a Monday morning, so I *get* to wake up extra early because I *get* to help my daughter get ready for school. I *get* to pack her a lunch and a snack for school. Then I *get* to do some laundry—the clothes are piling up! Next on my list, I *get* to work on an article for my business, and then I *get* to start prepping for a talk I have in a few days. There are some emails and calls I *get* to return. Phew! So much I *get* to do!

This version touches my heart and leaves me feeling grateful and upbeat. It helps me realize how fortunate I am to be able to do all these things, and it helps me appreciate all the good things in my life—my daughter, my business, my health, even my clothes, washing machine, and computer.

Give it a try. Write down all the things you *have* to do. Then switch out the words so it says all the things you *get* to do. Notice a difference? If you need an even bigger shift, imagine something in your life has happened so that you aren't able to do the things on your list. Now you would switch the words from "have to" to "don't get to."

I would like to thank my dear friend Jen Wilson of New Leaf Coaching for sharing this powerful insight with me.

_____

_____

_____

_____

_____

_____

_____

_____

_____

_____

_____

_____

_____

_____

_____

_____

_____

_____

_____

_____

_____

_____

_____

## 42. Feeling Overwhelmed Trying to Do It All
*Being realistic and adjusting your expectations*

This post is dedicated to a wonderful friend whom I so greatly admire. She's a superhero—incredibly busy in her successful business, a dedicated mom with small children, *and* she maintains a challenging exercise regime. She puts me to shame in the amazing amount of stuff she accomplishes in a week. Yet she struggles with overwhelm and feelings of not doing enough, just like me.

Have you ever noticed how many of us think we need to do it all ourselves, help everybody and be everything? After all, with today's technology and conveniences, we can get so much more done, more quickly. We say yes too often, like when we're asked to join committees or projects at work and within our communities. We find ourselves (and our kids) involved in multiple activities. We spend a lot of effort trying to be a good employee, boss, parent, partner, etc.

However, all this running and stretching ourselves thin leads to higher expectations and more distractions instead of feelings of greater accomplishment. Our lives are busier and crazier than ever. Yet we're still overwhelmed because we can't get everything on our to-do lists done.

Let's face it—we *can't* do it all! Instead, we *can* lower our expectations of what we can reasonably accomplish in a day. We *can* go easy on ourselves when we just can't seem to get everything done we had planned. We can get better at saying no when someone asks us to be part of another activity. Most importantly, we *can* look back and celebrate the things we *did* get done. This approach takes practice and intention because it goes against our cultural conditioning of always "doing." Maybe we should add these to our to-do list?!

Think of all the things you need to do. Are your expectations reasonable? What have you already finished that you can celebrate? How can you remember this practice during particularly busy times?

_____

_____

_____

_____

_____

_____

_____

_____

_____

_____

_____

_____

_____

_____

_____

_____

_____

_____

_____

_____

_____

# 43. Being Thankful While You Wait
*Using the extra time for gratitude instead of frustration*

Don't you just hate waiting? I get so impatient! It seems like such a waste of time when I have so many things I need to do. My biggest pet peeves are waiting on hold to get a customer service person or getting stuck in a traffic jam. I find myself getting more and more frustrated as I wait.

After learning more from Positive Psychology, I realized I could shift my perspective. Instead of thinking of waiting as an inconvenience—or worse—I could think of it as a mini break from my normally busy schedule. I could use this break as an opportunity to take time for something positive such as a quick gratitude practice.

So now, when I'm waiting:

- for a red light,
- in line at the drive-through,
- in line at the checkout,
- on hold on the phone,
- at the doctor's office,
- in a traffic jam,

I use it as a reminder to be grateful (see Tip 16). If I'm in my car, I think about how grateful I am that the price of gas is so low, that I have a reliable vehicle to drive, that I can adjust the temperature in my car to be comfortable, that I enjoy where I live, etc. This in-the-moment approach works better *for me* than keeping a gratitude journal.

When I practice a little gratitude while I wait, it lifts my spirits and makes the wait seem much shorter. I'm reinforcing those positive neural pathways in my brain, so it will continue to get easier to notice the good—even while

I wait. It's not a waste of time after all!

What are some situations where you find yourself waiting? How could you use this time to shift your thinking? Make a list of examples where you find yourself waiting and reasons to be grateful in those situations.

_____

_____

_____

_____

_____

_____

_____

_____

_____

_____

_____

_____

_____

_____

_____

_____

_____

_____

_____

_____

# 44. Life Can Seem so Unfair!
## *Finding opportunities to learn and grow*

Maybe you've had situations in your life that just didn't seem fair. But what if life isn't supposed to be fair? Or perfect? Or even easy? What if, instead, life is a place to learn and grow? I know, I know! Why do learning and growing have to be *painful*? Yet we tend to remember the lesson if the pain is memorable.

The idea that life's pain may genuinely be helpful was a real shift in perspective for me. It's not something I can always remember, but what a difference it's made! The biggest change I've seen is when something doesn't go the way I want. I can now recover much faster. For example, during a trip I made to Canada to do a workshop for a company, I was surprised that I was delayed in customs. It turns out there had been recent changes in legislation that required extra paperwork and fees for me and the company that hired me. I had to make several calls back and forth with the company. And, because my cell phone didn't work in Canada, it also meant extra taxi trips from the customs office to my hotel so I could use the phone in my room.

During this hectic morning, I reminded myself that life is not supposed to be fair. This situation was an excellent opportunity to practice creating my own experience in these stressful circumstances. I could only do what I could do. So I joked around with the customs officer and people-watched in the airport. I didn't stress. In the end, everything worked out. I was able to make it to my workshop on time feeling calm. Phew!

I recently saw this quote by author Jackson Kiddard that fits this theme so well—

> *"Anything that annoys you is for teaching you patience.*
> *Anyone who abandons you is for teaching you how to*

*stand up on your own two feet.*
*Anything that angers you is for teaching you forgiveness and compassion.*
*Anything that has power over you is for teaching you*
*how to take your power back.*
*Anything you hate is for teaching you unconditional love.*
*Anything you fear is for teaching you courage to overcome your fear.*
*Anything you can't control is for teaching you how to*
*let go and trust the Universe."*

Think back on your life. What experiences, painful or otherwise, have taught you patience, self-confidence, forgiveness, or courage?

_____

_____

_____

_____

_____

_____

_____

_____

_____

_____

_____

_____

_____

_____

_____

# 45. Different Ways to View Your Day
*Switching your perspective for less stress*

Here's one way to look at my Wednesday:

I had lost track of time and now only had 10 minutes to drive through downtown to my next meeting! I was going to be late for a seminar I was giving for a client. With my adrenaline flowing and my heart pumping, I grabbed my bag and raced to my car. Even though the client's place was close by, I was very stressed because I had to navigate confusing one-way streets and find a place to park in the crowded downtown.

As I got close, I spotted a parking garage, so I pulled in. I circled impatiently, but couldn't see an open spot. Frustrated, I left the garage and quickly pulled into a parking space on the street, only to find that it had a meter that required change. I put in every quarter and dime I had, but it wasn't enough. Darn! I searched my car for more change. I found some, but the time on the meter was going to be cutting it close. I rushed, breathless, into the conference center 15 minutes later than planned to get ready to present.

But there's another way of looking at this:

I had lost track of time because I was having such an enjoyable conversation in my previous meeting. Using my GPS, I was able to get to the next place without a single wrong turn, despite the confusing one-way streets. The parking garage was full, but as soon as I pulled out, I was grateful to find a space right away on the street. The meter didn't take credit cards, and I didn't have enough quarters in my purse. But I was fortunate to find a few more in my car that got me close to the time I thought I needed.

Even though I arrived later than planned, I was relieved to realize I still had plenty of time to get ready for my presentation. And when I returned to my car after the program, I saw the parking police walking down the other side of the street. Sure enough, the meter was expired, but I was thankful that I could get to my car before I got a ticket.

Was it a good day or a bad day? All of these things happened to me, but what aspects would I choose to focus on? I decided it was a great day with some valuable lessons.

Have you ever experienced a time when it seemed like everything was going wrong? How did it turn out in the end? Which parts did you or could you have focused on to make it a good day?

_____

_____

_____

_____

_____

_____

_____

_____

_____

_____

_____

_____

_____

_____

_____

_____

# 46. Don't Reduce Your Stress— Use Your Stress

*Shifting your thoughts about the hazards of stress*

Are you stressed about being stressed? We hear a lot of talk about how all of the stress in our lives is bad for our health. It's easy to find tips and strategies on reducing our stress. But what if there is more to the story? In fact, recently there's been some amazing research that shows it's more important to pay attention to our *attitude* about our stress. If we *think* stress is bad for us, there's a good chance it will be.

Let me tell you about a study with 3,000 individuals in the United States.[40] These people were asked two questions:

1.  How much stress have you experienced in the past year?
2.  Do you believe stress is harmful to your health?

Eight years later, they looked at how many people had died.

The results were stunning! The people who indicated they had experienced high levels of stress *and* believed stress was harmful had a 43% increased risk of dying. What's so stunning? The people who indicated they had experienced high levels of stress and *didn't* believe stress was bad had *no* increased death risk. In fact, their risk was less than any group in the study, including those who said they had very little stress in their lives.

Additional research has found that when we shift our thoughts to believing that stress is valuable for energizing our bodies and preparing us to face challenges, it not only changes our mental attitude about stress, it literally changes the way our bodies react to it. Our physiological response to stress now looks similar to feelings of joy or courage. For example, our heart rate still increases, but our blood vessels don't constrict.[41] For more details, check out author and psychologist Kelly McGonigal's TED talk.[42]

According to McGonigal, "How you think about stress matters." Maybe it's time to rethink your views on stress. Reflect on what's stressing you out now. How can you see it as useful?

_____

_____

_____

_____

_____

_____

_____

_____

_____

_____

_____

_____

_____

_____

_____

_____

_____

_____

_____

_____

_____

## 47. Changing the Stories We Tell Ourselves
*Are you jumping to the worst conclusion?*

We don't observe the world around us—we "interpret" it. We take a piece of information, make a bunch of assumptions, and then jump to a conclusion. We may even add additional content without knowing if it's true, just to support our story. Why is this a problem? Because our brains are wired to anticipate the worst.

When our friend doesn't call or text us back within their usual timeframe, we may assume something's wrong. Are they mad at us? What did we do to make them mad? They have no right to be mad! Or how about when that driver cuts us off on the highway? We might assume that they're a jerk and that they think they own the road.

There are many opportunities for our brains to jump to conclusions when we don't have enough information to know what's really going on. Our friend may have lost their phone. And that driver who cut us off? Well, perhaps they aren't familiar with this part of town, they're late for an appointment, *and* their kids are fighting in the back seat.

I've found an excellent tool to help me change my stories. It's called the ABCD approach. This version is based on a classic cognitive behavioral therapy (CBT) technique developed by one of the method's founders, Albert Ellis.[43]

- A is the **Action** that happened to you. Your colleague didn't get their part of the project done.

- B is your **Belief** about that action. You believe that your colleague isn't doing their job.

- C is the **Consequences** of your belief. You're mad at your colleague and think they're a slacker.

- D is for **Disputing** your belief—and that is that key to this process. Maybe your colleague isn't a slacker. Maybe work got unexpectedly busy, or a crisis came up that they had to deal with and didn't have time to get their other work done.

When we can remind ourselves that we don't have all the facts and are just jumping to conclusions, we can change the consequences—our emotions and reaction. This process gives us the opportunity to remain calm and gather more facts when possible. Or simply to realize we are assuming the worst when we may never know the truth—like the driver who cut you off.

Reflect on a past situation and the story you told yourself. How could you have applied the ABCD approach to change the narrative?

_____

_____

_____

_____

_____

_____

_____

_____

_____

_____

_____

_____

_____

_____

## 48. The Movie in Your Mind
*Don't get stuck replaying painful scenes*

Think of a favorite scene from a movie—preferably one filled with lots of emotion. The scene that comes to my mind is from *Forrest Gump*. Towards the end of the story, Forrest visits Jenny's apartment and finds out she's now a mom. Jenny tells him that the little boy's name is Forrest, after his daddy. As he suddenly realizes that this child is his, Forrest's brow furrows in deep concern and fear. He finally chokes out the question, "Is he smart or . . . is he like me?" He smiles in great relief to hear his son is indeed very smart.

Every time I watch that scene my heart fills with emotion, and I cry. It's just a movie, but it feels so real!

The same thing happens when we replay a past drama, hurt, or frustration in our minds. We get caught up in the emotion, as if it was occurring again right now, but it's not. It's just a movie playing inside our heads. Sure, it may have really happened, but that was in the past.

Why would we choose to suffer through it again? When we physically injure ourselves, like accidentally cutting a finger or stubbing a toe, it hurts for a little while and then the pain is gone. But as humans, when we experience an emotional hurt, we replay it over and over, sometimes hundreds of times and sometimes for years. This brooding is part of our survival instinct that's designed to help us avoid a similar pain in the future. But it can be easy to get stuck there.

The trick is to catch ourselves doing these replays. Then we can remind ourselves it's not real, it's just a scene from the past and dwelling on this memory isn't helping us. We can't change what happened. We *can* choose a different thought—something that will benefit us instead of making us suffer.

Some ideas for shifting our thoughts include focusing on gratitude, a favorite good memory, or even a favorite song. Sometimes it's helpful to distract ourselves by calling a friend, watching a funny video, or getting outside. Another option is to think of something you can do to help someone else. Try different things to find what works for you (see Tip 17).

What is your favorite way to avoid getting stuck in a painful scene? Think of a few ideas so you'll be prepared the next time you catch yourself replaying a bad memory.

_____

_____

_____

_____

_____

_____

_____

_____

_____

_____

_____

_____

_____

_____

_____

_____

_____

_____

_____

# 49. Defeating Discouragement
## *Don't let it steal your dreams*

I find discouragement can slowly creep in and take over my mood. Or it can suddenly hit me like a crashing wave. Either way, I feel heavy and dispirited, and I totally lose motivation. I feel like giving up. Has this ever happened to you? Some common triggers for me are an unexpected obstacle or something that doesn't go as smoothly as I expected.

Over the past couple of years, I've watched waves of discouragement hit my husband as he tackled a very different type of project. He's not a writer—he's a machinist—but he's been working on publishing a children's book about a story he made up for our daughter. His discouragement would vary, sometimes related to how long things were taking—"This is never going to get done! I should just quit now." Or "Why would anyone want to read something I wrote?"

Now the book is finally finished! Hooray! But the discouragement doesn't end. Just because you put a book on Amazon doesn't mean people will find it and buy it. So these days, the discouragement sounds like, "No one wants to read my book!" This feeling can be especially strong after he's done a promotion like a giveaway or an interview.

Despite the many times he wanted to give up, my husband stuck with it and persevered in finishing his book. Now, when he talks to elementary school classes about writing his book, he shares three lessons that he's learned:

- Don't give up on your dreams. It's not how smart you are but how good you are at persevering.

- Surround yourself with sources of inspiration to lift your spirits and keep you motivated. One of his favorites is the video of Heather Dorniden, the college track runner who takes a nasty fall during a 600-meter race, yet gets back up and, to everyone's utter amazement, wins!

- Don't be afraid to ask for help. When we run into an obstacle or just need some encouragement, we should reach out to others.

What situations have caused you to get discouraged? How can you apply the three lessons above the next time you feel like giving up?

_____

_____

_____

_____

_____

_____

_____

_____

_____

_____

_____

_____

_____

_____

_____

_____

_____

_____

_____

_____

# 50. Focusing on Energy Management
*A new perspective on work-life balance*

Do you ever feel like you're so busy, you don't have any time left for a life? Today's fast-paced, always-on world is continuously requiring us to do more and more, faster and faster. We hear a lot about work-life balance (see Tip 8) and time management. What if there's another approach?

I'm fascinated by the work of Jim Loehr and Tony Schwartz. In their book, "The Power of Full Engagement,"[44] they shift the paradigm by saying it's not our *time* we should focus on, but our *energy*. This concept is gaining a lot of attention. Here are a couple of examples that hit home for me. We know it's important to take time to be with our families, but if our energy has been totally zapped by our work, is it truly *quality* time? Or we may feel guilty if we take extra time during our day to go for a walk or chat with a friend, but what if that recharges our battery so we get more done? In their book, the authors point out, "The number of hours in a day is fixed, but the quantity and quality of energy available to us is not."

What can we do to get more energy?

* The first step is to be sure we're taking care of the basics: getting enough sleep (7-8 hours nightly), eating regular, healthy meals, and exercising.

* Data suggests that every 90-120 minutes, we should take a break to recharge. This could be standing up and stretching, taking several deep breaths, taking a quick walk through the hallways, stepping outside, or talking to a friend.

* Our energy level is also dependent on our mindset. We'll be more energized if we do more of what we do best *and* what we enjoy. We can have a talk with our boss about past projects we've liked and possible ways to delegate some tasks that drain our energy. We can get involved with special committees or projects we find interesting.

- We also need to be sure to schedule time for our families and ourselves. These should be fun and relaxing hours *without* digital connections to work.

- Finally, my favorite is that we need to stop wasting energy dwelling on things outside of our control, whether they're past frustrations or future worries. Just imagine what we could achieve if we took the energy we spent on things we cannot change and invested it in things we can!

What are some ways you could apply these tips to better manage your energy?

_____

_____

_____

_____

_____

_____

_____

_____

_____

_____

_____

_____

_____

_____

_____

_____

*Section 3:*

---

# BUILDING
# POSITIVE
# RELATIONSHIPS

# 51. Responding to Other People's Negativity
*Tips for maintaining your positivity in challenging relationships*

When I ask people what causes the most negativity in their life, the overwhelming response is *other people*. In fact, a common question I get after my talks on positivity goes something like this. "I'm trying to be more positive, but my partner/coworker/parent is so negative. How can I get them to change?"

This can be a very challenging and frustrating situation. As you try to see more of the good in your life and work, you have someone who's constantly pointing out the bad. One thing here is very clear. The only person you can change is yourself. So what can you do?

If possible, limit the time you spend with the negative person. This approach may sound mean, but it's important to surround yourself with people who lift you up and boost your spirits. On the other hand, if it's someone who's an integral part of your life, such as a partner, family member, or a coworker you need to interact with, consider these strategies:

- Balance out their negativity by noticing other positive things in your life or work to keep your positivity up (see Tips 6 and 17).

- Do your best to see and focus on their good traits. Maybe they assume the worst, but maybe they're also very helpful or have a good sense of humor.

- Realize that you can't change them. Be aware that some of their attitude is due to their life experiences, and a significant portion is actually due to their genetics. See if you can feel compassion for them.

- When they bring up negative topics, listen, and, if possible, validate their feelings, but don't encourage the conversation by joining in with additional negative comments or questions.

- Remember that other people's words and actions are about them and their problems. Whatever negativity they aim at us is really a result of their own issues. "People who are not happy with themselves cannot possibly be happy with you."—author unknown

The interesting thing is when you accept them for the way they are, you may find that they don't seem quite so difficult to be around. They may also sense a change in your attitude towards them, which can affect how they interact with you.

Reflect on how you could use this approach with someone in your life. What specific actions can you take?

_____

_____

_____

_____

_____

_____

_____

_____

_____

_____

_____

_____

## 52. Why Are Some People More Positive Than Others?
*Positivity is in our genes*

Many people are shocked by one of the fascinating pieces of research from Positive Psychology that I commonly share in my talks. After my programs, people tell me how it totally changed the way they think about their life and how they view others. In fact, a year after attending one of my presentations, a gentleman who made several comments defending the benefits of negativity, told me how a single piece of information I shared flipped his attitude. He said he's now happier than he ever imagined.

This eye-opening insight comes from studies on fraternal and identical twins.[45] Identical twins that share the same DNA have strikingly similar levels of positivity, even if they were separated at birth and grew up in very different circumstances. This phenomenon doesn't apply to fraternal twins who, by definition, have different DNA. After hundreds of these studies, scientists estimate that about 50% of our ability to "see the glass as half-full" is due to our genetics![46]

It wasn't until sometime in my 30s that I started to realize that I think about and notice the good things in life more easily than many other people. Learning about the twins studies helped me understand that this is at least partially because I inherited positive genes. A few individuals in my life didn't seem to be so lucky. They weren't *trying* to be negative—they were being influenced by their genetics. Suddenly, I understood that I should be less critical and more understanding of their emotions.

Another insight that came out of the twins studies is that roughly 40% of our ability to be positive is due to *how we think*. This discovery is truly powerful because it means we *do* have control— we *can* take steps to build our positivity and change how we experience our lives. The problem is that most people aren't aware of this possibility. The idea that we can train our minds to shift how we think is a relatively new concept in the science field.

Reflect on how knowing this information might impact the way you view one or more people in your life that have a different level of positivity than you. How does it affect how you view yourself?

_____

_____

_____

_____

_____

_____

_____

_____

_____

_____

_____

_____

_____

_____

_____

_____

_____

_____

_____

_____

_____

_____

_____

# 53. Communicating That You Care
*Are you choosing the right language?*

If you want to show your partner how much you love them, you might decide to buy them a little something special at the store—maybe their favorite candy. They might think it's nice, but what if they don't see this gift as a sign of your love because what they really want is some quality time with you? But because you're so busy, they feel neglected and unappreciated. The problem may be that you have different love languages.

We all have different personalities, values, life experiences, and ways of thinking, but there is another critical area where our differences impact our personal relationships and even our work experiences. It's important to understand our language and the language that others have for feeling loved, cared for, and appreciated.

Carol Rogers, the famous humanistic psychologist, said one of our core humans needs is to feel valued, respected, and loved. Here's where it gets interesting because what makes one person feel valued and loved may be different from another. You can see how this can cause trouble with our relationships. Dr. Gary Chapman in his book, *The 5 Love Languages* (also see *The 5 Languages of Appreciation in the Workplace*), defines these languages as:[47]

- **Words of Affirmation:** Saying, "Thanks for washing the dishes. I appreciate your help."

- **Acts of Service:** Folding the laundry or putting gas in the car

- **Receiving Gifts:** Giving a thoughtful card or small gift

- **Quality Time:** Making a date to watch a movie or go for a walk together

- *Physical Touch:* Giving hugs, kisses, high fives, fist bumps

One approach is to ask your partner or child for past examples of when they felt loved. Another sign is to notice which language they use to show you *their* love. We usually use the language we prefer to receive. You can also identify your love language at www.5lovelanguages.com.

Which love language do you prefer? What about your partner, child, or other family members? What can you do to show them that you care using their language?

_____

_____

_____

_____

_____

_____

_____

_____

_____

_____

_____

_____

_____

_____

_____

_____

_____

_____

## 54. Watch Out for These Five Triggers
*Social situations that can set off our natural threat responses*

I received an email from a coworker from another department. They weren't happy with how I was handling a situation with a customer. Though irritated, I politely responded, explaining my reasoning. The co-worker replied, continuing to challenge my actions, *and they copied my boss*. What? I was *furious*! That was uncalled for!

Isn't it interesting how an action that questions our judgment and expertise can trigger such a strong response? Now, in hindsight, I understand that my status had been threatened. My natural survival instincts had kicked in as if I were in actual physical danger. Watch out!

Interestingly, studies by David Rock of the Neuroleadership Institute and others have found five social situations that can have this type of effect.[48] His **SCARF** model highlights social interactions known to trigger the threat or reward response in our brains. Such threat situations include:

- **Status:** Situations that challenge our social or professional standing.

- **Certainty:** Situations where we feel uncertain and feel we don't have all the information we need.

- **Autonomy:** Situations where we don't feel in control and feel we don't have choices.

- **Relatedness:** Situations where we don't feel a connection with the other person; they seem very different in their ideas or appearance.

- **Fairness:** Situations where we've been mistreated or have been accused of being unfair.

Why is this important to know? Whether it's interactions with our colleagues, friends, or family, it's very helpful to be aware of these triggers so we can avoid saying or doing something to set off the other person's threat response. It's also valuable to recognize our own strong reactions and realize it's our survival instincts kicking in.

Can you remember a time when you triggered one of these threat responses in someone or when you had a response? What could you do differently?

_____

_____

_____

_____

_____

_____

_____

_____

_____

_____

_____

_____

_____

_____

_____

_____

_____

_____

# 55. Personality Styles
## *Understanding and appreciating our differences*

**"S**eriously, you don't like chocolate? How is that possible?" Yet here was my friend, telling me they didn't like the taste. I was confused and couldn't understand why they didn't share my love of this wonderful treat. Have you ever been talking to someone and found that they have a very different preference or priority than you? Maybe it's around politics or religion. Or it could be something subtle, like the way you approach a problem or even how you do the dishes.

What I've learned and what is incredibly helpful to understand is that it's totally normal to have different preferences and ideas than other people. A large part of these are personality differences due to genetics.[49] Some of us are very direct, while some are more reserved and cautious. Some of us prefer to focus on getting things done while others are more concerned about how other people are affected.

A former boss in my corporate job would send me one- or two-word emails. I assumed he was upset with me. Then we took a personality assessment, and I found out that was just *his style*. He was naturally direct and action-oriented. It had nothing to do with me.

I've been fortunate to have the chance to learn about the different personality styles. Here are some important insights I've gained:

- One personality style is not better than another, although we may tend to think ours is the best. Each one is valuable with its own strengths and challenges.

- Understanding our own personality can give us insights into how others perceive us.

- Knowing someone else's personality can give us a deeper understanding of their preferences and perspective (like short emails).

- Once we know their style, we can then adapt our behavior to better connect and communicate with them, making our interactions easier.

I believe if we could understand and appreciate other people's personalities, we would have more peace in our relationships, our work, and even in the world.

Think of someone in your life who has different ideas and preferences than you because they have a different style. How might your interactions and attitude change if you were more accepting of their differences, remembering that it's just part of their personality?

_____

_____

_____

_____

_____

_____

_____

_____

_____

_____

_____

_____

_____

_____

# 56. Cortisol Demons
*Don't get triggered by other people's stress*

When we experience negative emotions like anxiety or frustration, it triggers the release of cortisol in our body. Cortisol then increases our sensitivity to other stressors and keeps us focused on the problem. We can get so focused, in fact, that we lose perspective and the ability to even think logically about other things. It's much easier to notice this happening to someone else rather than ourselves. The other person may act unreasonable and say things that put us on the defensive. When this happens, what should we do? Our instinctive response is nicely highlighted by this great parable.

The King is away the day that a nasty demon visits the castle. The demon jauntily strides right up to the King's throne and takes a seat. The King's knights are aghast! How dare this demon have such gall! They start yelling at him to leave, which only makes the demon even nastier. He starts screaming obscenities back at the knights. The knights prod the demon with their swords and yell even louder. The demon becomes smellier, uglier, and bigger. The knights get angrier and angrier as the demon grows in size.

Finally, the King returns and sees the terrible situation that's taking place. He is very wise and quickly calls off his knights. He then turns to the demon and asks how he can help him. The demon becomes quieter. The King continues in a calm voice and offers to bring the demon something to drink. The demon starts to shrink. As the King continues to treat the demon with kindness, the demon starts shriveling up until—poof!—he disappears entirely.

When we interact with someone who's flooded in cortisol, they may say or do something that makes *us* upset and triggers *our* cortisol cycle. The result isn't pretty! Our instinct is to attack back, which only makes the demon grow bigger. Instead, we can recognize what's happening and diffuse the situation by asking, "Is everything OK?"

Keep an *eye* out for cortisol demons and see if you can prevent the counter-attack. Can you think of past situations where you could have tried this approach? Are there potential future situations where this information could be useful?

_____

_____

_____

_____

_____

_____

_____

_____

_____

_____

_____

_____

_____

_____

_____

_____

_____

_____

_____

_____

_____

_____

## 57. Is Someone Bugging You?
*Changing your reaction is easier than changing other people*

Ever notice how once you focus on something that bugs you about someone, everything they do starts to irritate you? It seems like the only things you can see are their faults. Then this feeling starts to affect how you treat them, which only makes them behave in a way that frustrates you even more. It can become a vicious cycle.

I know you've heard this many times, but it can be hard to remember and difficult to apply: *The one person you can control is yourself.* Accepting other people as they are is easy when they're agreeable. But when they don't behave, think, or feel the way we expect, it can drive us crazy and cause countless problems in our relationships. We believe that *they* should change to match *our* expectations. I'm not saying we can't influence people. But that usually requires building a relationship based on trust and then modeling the behavior we would like to see.

So what if *we* changed the way we thought about these challenging interactions? Instead of getting frustrated, we can:

- Remember that no one is perfect, including us.

- Understand that our brains are wired to focus on the negative—it's our natural default mode to see their faults.

- Recognize that this person has many good traits—maybe even some we don't have. Make and keep a running list of the good things about the other person. Add to it every week so you're on the lookout for their positive qualities.

- Consider that we can learn patience and tolerance from interacting with people who have different perspectives than ours.

- Realize that we don't know what current situation may be causing their stress or unhappiness.

- Appreciate that we may not be aware of their history, ways they've been hurt, or what the little voice in their head is telling them.

There's a story of a great spiritual teacher that traveled the countryside, visiting different villages with his entourage of helpers. One of these helpers was a very grouchy cook. When people asked the teacher why he kept such an ornery grump around, he would say, "He's *my* teacher."

How would our lives—and even the world—improve if we worked on changing our *reactions* to others instead of trying to *change* others? We don't have to agree with or condone their actions. But we can invest our energy in the one person we can change, ourselves. Reflect on how you could use the strategies listed above to help manage your frustration with someone who's bugging you.

_____

_____

_____

_____

_____

_____

_____

_____

_____

_____

_____

_____

_____

## 58. You Disagree? How Interesting!
*Using curiosity to override defensiveness*

We each have *different* life experiences and *different* personalities that contribute to our *different* perspectives. No wonder we have *different* ideas compared to other people in our lives. Deep down, we know this individual uniqueness is good, but when we disagree with someone, we can feel frustrated that they don't see things our way. In our frustration, we may say things or use a certain tone of voice that only makes the situation worse. This is because we're wired to *react* instead of choosing our responses, *and* we instinctively believe we're right. As you probably know, this knee-jerk reaction can cause endless problems in our work and home lives.

How can we put aside our differences and our need to be right? Wouldn't it be better, instead of getting defensive, to think, *How interesting! How interesting that I'm reacting and feeling this way. How interesting that they have different ideas. Let me be curious and ask questions to help me understand their point of view.* When we choose this open-minded approach, it not only makes it easier and more fun to communicate and collaborate—we end up discovering more opportunities and better ways of doing things.

I know firsthand how hard this can be, especially in the heat of the moment when my emotions are running strong. It's so easy to react instead of taking the time and energy to think about how I want to respond. One day I was talking with my husband about a little woodworking project I wanted him to do. He didn't like my approach and was telling me how he thought it should be done. I noticed myself getting defensive and irritated. I knew my approach was better. Why couldn't he see it my way?

I struggled but managed to tune in and notice how I was reacting. *Hmmm, How interesting that I'm feeling triggered by his difference in opinion. How interesting that he has a different idea of how to do this project.* It definitely helped me avoid getting more upset and allowed me to stay somewhat calm so I could act reasonably. In the end, I could see why he preferred his approach.

Can you think of any recent interactions that would have had a better outcome by thinking, *How interesting?* Is there an upcoming situation that you know will be challenging where this approach might help?

_____

_____

_____

_____

_____

_____

_____

_____

_____

_____

_____

_____

_____

_____

_____

_____

_____

_____

_____

# 59. You Got a Raise? How Nice!
*Your response to others' good news matters*

How do you react when someone shares good news with you? Social psychologist Shelly Gable of UCLA found that the health of your relationship with another person—especially your partner—relies on your response.[50] In fact, how you respond to their good news is even more important than when they share something bad. When I first learned this, I was shocked! We've all heard how it's important to listen and sympathize when another person is upset to show that you care. The idea that what we say when they have *exciting* news matters more seemed, well . . . unusual.

Gable has studied close relationships for years. She's found that, out of four possible ways to respond to a partner's positive news, only one—an "active-constructive response"—is good. A negative or semi-positive reaction can undermine trust and satisfaction.

Let's say your partner comes home and excitedly shares that they just got a raise. Here's how *not* to respond:

- **Active-destructive:** Frown. "Well, it's about time! They should have given you a raise last year. I bet your raise is less than what (name of other person) got."

- **Passive-destructive:** No expression. "Did you remember to get milk on your way home?"

- **Passive-constructive:** Smile. "That's great. By the way, do we have plans for this weekend? I want to meet my friend for lunch."

Here's how to build connection, trust and positive wellbeing for both sides:

- **Active-constructive:** Smile. Stop what you're doing. Make eye contact. "How exciting! I'm so happy for you! Tell me more. What did they say?"

Showing genuine interest and asking questions builds on the positive moment and can create an upward spiral. This is true not only for our intimate relationships but also with our kids and coworkers.

How did you respond the last time someone shared something they were excited about? What can you do next time?

_____

_____

_____

_____

_____

_____

_____

_____

_____

_____

_____

_____

_____

_____

_____

_____

_____

_____

_____

# 60. I Don't Want Your Advice!
## *Overriding your defensive instinct*

Darn! I had just missed the turn to take my daughter to camp, and now we were going to be late. *Darn! Darn! Darn! Being late makes me feel stressed!*

My daughter started teasing me about being forgetful, so I explained I was feeling anxious—and distracted—because I had a lot of things to get done that day. After lamenting about my long list, she asked which of those I *had* to get done today. She then lectured me on setting priorities and not creating unneeded stress. Did I mention she's 10? It was hard to say, "You're right." I wanted to say, "What do you know!" or "I don't need this right now!" Yet if I want her to be open to my "input," I knew I had to stay open to hers. So I took a long breath and paused. How do I want to respond in this situation? Fighting my defensive instincts, I smiled and said, "Thank you. You have a good point."

A common truth is that it's much easier to advise than to receive advice. How can we stay open and realize that these people are sharing their thoughts out of goodwill and not to make us defensive? Whether or not you like their advice, here's something to try.

- Realize it's instinctive and normal to get defensive when someone is correcting or advising us.

- Notice your reaction and how it makes you feel.

- Pause and remind yourself that you can override your instinctive reaction.

- Think of how you would respond to a small child or grandparent. We tend to have more patience with them.

- Remind yourself to speak with intention.

- Practice this approach in easy situations. It takes time to get good at it.

Think of a past situation where you became impatient with someone's attempt to offer their "help." What could you have done or said differently based on the steps above?

_____

_____

_____

_____

_____

_____

_____

_____

_____

_____

_____

_____

_____

_____

_____

_____

_____

_____

_____

_____

# 61. Permission to Be Human
*Adding a link to the chain of forgiveness, starting with yourself*

I couldn't believe it! I had the appointment in my calendar, but for some reason, I'd totally overlooked it. Now, I had missed it completely and had left the other person waiting. I felt terrible! Did they think I was just a thoughtless person who had blown them off? How could I make it up to them?

Has this ever happened to you? I'm the type of person who can easily spend a lot of time berating myself for making mistakes like this, yet I know that won't change what happened. Now I work harder at forgiving myself and looking for what I can learn. For example:

- *How can this mistake help me grow?* I can look at it as an opportunity to practice self-forgiveness. I can remember that beating myself up won't undo what happened. Of course, I can apologize or offer some way to make amends, but making myself miserable doesn't help the situation.

- *What can I do differently in the future?* For this example, I can develop a habit of checking my calendar more carefully and leaving myself reminders if there's something in my schedule I think I might forget.

- *How can this help me relate to others better?* The next time someone else makes a mistake that impacts my schedule, I can remember that no one is perfect, including me.

My Positive Psychology teacher, Tal Ben-Shahar, has a saying that I love— "Give yourself and others permission to be human."

We all make mistakes, so we shouldn't be too hard on ourselves or others when they happen. Sometimes these mishaps can be very serious or hurtful and cause us or others pain. However, if we're resilient, we can grow and learn from these experiences. It reminds me of a quote from the Sufi poet Rumi—"How can you be polished if you are irritated by every rub?"

When we forgive ourselves, we're more able to forgive others. When we forgive others, *they're* more able to forgive others. Be the next link in the chain of forgiveness.

What's an example of a recent mistake you or another person made that you could use to practice forgiveness?

_____

_____

_____

_____

_____

_____

_____

_____

_____

_____

_____

_____

_____

_____

_____

_____

_____

# 62. Feeling Unappreciated?
*Try pointing out your contributions*

D o you ever feel like all of the things you do go unnoticed, and no one says thank you? Does this happen at work? At home? I've definitely struggled with this in multiple situations. When I feel like I'm being taken for granted, it puts me in a bad mood. I get frustrated, impatient, and I'm not much fun to be around. In the past when this happened, I didn't like how it made me feel, but I didn't know what to do about it.

Then I learned this simple—but not easy—tool. Instead of expecting others to read my mind and notice the things I've done, I simply *tell* them. The trick is to say something *before* we're feeling unappreciated and *before* we get upset. Why? If we wait until we're frustrated, we'll be in attack mode, making the other person feel defensive. This is never helpful and just makes matters worse. But if we tell them in a kind and calm voice, "I was really glad I was able to finish cleaning the kitchen this morning. Did you notice how nice it looks?" Or "That project took a lot of work, but I was happy with how it turned out. What do you think?"

Pointing out our efforts and *asking* for appreciation and feedback may feel uncomfortable at first—especially with our boss. I know it still is for me. But when we calmly and gently let people know what we've done and prompt them for some recognition, we take back responsibility for the situation instead of just being a victim and feeling upset. When I hesitate at the idea of bringing up some task I've done, I tell myself that if I can't ask for acknowledgement then it can't be that important, and I shouldn't feel bad if they don't notice.

Another option I've found that can make it easier is to let others know that *you* don't always notice all the things *they* do. Tell them to feel free to point out the stuff that they've done because you want to show your appreciation.

As they see you doing it, they'll feel more comfortable saying something so both of you will have opportunities to acknowledge each other's great work.

What's an easy situation where you could try this approach this week?

_____

_____

_____

_____

_____

_____

_____

_____

_____

_____

_____

_____

_____

_____

_____

_____

_____

_____

_____

_____

_____

_____

# 63. And I Thought the Traffic Jam Was Bad!
## *Choosing your response to other people's reactions*

I had an interesting and educational experience while we were driving home from visiting family one weekend. About an hour from home, we ran into a major traffic jam on the interstate. Traffic was stopped or barely crawling. My husband was driving and seemed to be handling the frustration fairly well, but I was very surprised to hear my 10-year-old daughter spouting out her extreme irritation from the back seat. She continued to loudly voice her thoughts and share how upset she was. I wondered why it bothered her since she wasn't even the one driving.

As the minutes ticked by and there was no end to the delay in sight, I found I could accept that the traffic was out of my control, but I was becoming annoyed at my daughter's non-stop rant. We even commented that it's one thing to be annoyed and another to be *annoying*. I tried to slip in a remark about "choosing our experience," but she's highly tuned into any attempt I make at pointing out the positive. "Moooooooom! Stop with the positive stuff, already! OK?"

Then it hit me. I not only had the freedom to choose my response to the traffic jam, I could also choose how I responded to *her response*. We often tell ourselves that other people have *made* us frustrated or angry when the painful truth is that we've *let* them trigger our emotions. As I remembered this difficult adage, I reminded myself to take several deep breaths and not let myself get caught up in the drama.

What a good lesson! When we're in a stressful situation, we not only need to choose our attitude towards the circumstances but also towards how people around us are reacting. This can be tricky and may require even more effort and willpower on our part.

Can you think of a past experience where you were frustrated by the reaction of other people? How could you have noticed and changed your reaction to them?

_____

_____

_____

_____

_____

_____

_____

_____

_____

_____

_____

_____

_____

_____

_____

_____

_____

_____

_____

# 64. No One Is Perfect
*Appreciating the dents and scratches we all have*

My daughter has had the same stuffed toy ducky since her baby shower before she was born. She's slept with it every night for the past 11 years. It's worn, faded, and has a few holes, but she would never want it replaced with a new one. She loves its imperfections. It's exactly the way it's supposed to be.

As I was looking at the worn state of her ducky, it hit me. What if we could feel the same way about the imperfections of the *people* in our lives? Wouldn't it be nice if we could accept and love them just the way they are, despite the bruises and raw spots from the wear and tear of their life experiences? We may think they make bad decisions about their relationships, their money, or their life in general. We may feel like they're too sensitive, too self-centered, too driven, or too laid back. It's always easier to see what other people should do differently than it is to use that *same energy* to work on improving ourselves, even when we know that no one is perfect, including us.

This approach can even be helpful for feeling more acceptance and compassion towards people we no longer interact with in our daily lives because they live far away or because they've passed away.

So, let's try an experiment. Just for fun, choose someone in your life that's easy for you to criticize. Decide that you're going to accept their imperfections—that they are exactly who they're supposed to be. This doesn't mean you have to agree with or like their behavior or attitude. You're just appreciating that they're a fellow human being who has some dents and scratches from being banged up in life. Reflect on how this might affect what you say or do around them.

Remember this thought every time you interact with this person. It may be helpful to write it down somewhere you'll see it so you don't forget. After a few times, notice how you feel and how they respond. Has anything changed?

Once, a gentleman in one of my audiences handed me a card that had an interesting twist on the original serenity prayer by Reinhold Niebuhr.

*"God, grant me the serenity*
*To accept the people I cannot change,*
*Courage to change the one I can,*
*And the wisdom to know it's me."*

_____

_____

_____

_____

_____

_____

_____

_____

_____

_____

_____

_____

_____

_____

_____

_____

# 65. Social Connections Are Good for You
*Making time for friends in a busy world*

Every day it seems like there are so many things I need to do. There are projects, paperwork, errands, etc. related to my work, my family, my home . . . It never ends! There just doesn't seem to be enough time left over to spend with friends. Do you ever feel this way?

When friends call me, it's tempting to say, "No, sorry. I'm too busy." Sometimes I struggle more than others because it feels self-indulgent to take time away from things I think I *should* be doing instead.

But I've learned from Positive Psychology and personal experience that the time I purposely set aside to spend with my wonderful friends is so important. It fuels my soul, charges my battery, and awakens my heart. I learn and grow when I'm with my friends. I know this is valuable time that I'm investing in my wellbeing. And I'm always glad I took the time to connect with them.

Studies show that strong social networks are important for both our physical and mental wellbeing. A study led by social psychologist James House from the University of Michigan found that not having quality social connections is harder on our health than obesity, smoking, and high blood pressure.[51] A meta-analysis of 148 studies with more than 300,000 participants from Brigham Young University suggests that strong social connections can increase our longevity by 50%.[52]

When I first learned about the important connection between our wellbeing and our social networks, I was concerned. I'm an introvert and find spending time with a large group of people exhausting. I need my alone time. Did this mean I wasn't getting the full benefit from the time I spent with friends? Then I read that the *quality* of our social contacts are more important than the quantity.[53] Phew!

Growing amounts of research demonstrate that we are very social creatures. We may think we want more money, power, fame, or beauty, but at
the root of most of these desires is our human need to belong and connect
with others.[54]

Think of the people in your life that you'd like to spend more time with.
What can you do or change to make it happen?

_____

_____

_____

_____

_____

_____

_____

_____

_____

_____

_____

_____

_____

_____

_____

_____

_____

_____

# 66. People Problems
*Interacting with unreasonable people*

M any studies tell us that the connections we have with the people in
our lives play critical roles in our physical and mental wellbeing.[51-54]
Yet it's easy to see that although our relationships can bring us joy, they can
also bring us plenty of frustration and heartache. I often recommend the
strategy of thinking, *How interesting!* when we encounter disagreements or
potential conflict (see Tip 58). That practice assumes we are dealing with
*reasonable* people who are also interested in resolving the conflict. What
about interactions with *unreasonable* people?

If you haven't read the book *How to Solve Your People Problems* by Dr. Alan
Godwin, you should pick up a copy.[55] We all have unreasonable people in
our lives and, yet, few of us know how to best deal with them. What makes
someone unreasonable? They are consistently *not* interested in solving
problems—their only interest is in being right because they have an irra-
tional aversion to being wrong. Godwin points out, "They automatically
assume we're the ones in the wrong, they fail to see their contributions
to the conflict, they claim no responsibility for any part of the problem,
they're not bothered by the impact of their words and actions on us, and
they change nothing because nothing about them needs changing."

Unreasonable people will often manipulate us to play a role in their drama.
They need us to agree with them, which can be extremely exhausting and
frustrating. Sound familiar?

The book explains that the solution to dealing with challenging people is to
stay calm and resist participating in their drama. If we recognize them for
who they are, we can adjust our expectations, knowing we cannot reason
with them. Then, we can avoid getting emotionally triggered when they
behave badly. We need to set boundaries in these relationships and realize
that our interactions will likely have limited depth, value, and growth.

Think of an unreasonable person in your life, someone who can never admit to being wrong and is constantly creating drama. How can this information help you in that relationship?

_____

_____

_____

_____

_____

_____

_____

_____

_____

_____

_____

_____

_____

_____

_____

_____

_____

_____

_____

_____

_____

_____

# 67. Being Kind vs. Being Right
*There's a time and place for each*

Are there times it's more important to be kind than right? I remember a scene from a TV show where a kid in the back seat of a car was smugly correcting his mom about some comment she'd made. His dad looked at him in the mirror and softly said, "Sometimes it's better to be kind than right."

That scene has stuck with me. As humans, we generally have an innate need to be right. I know I suffer from this. I can remember times arguing about some trivial detail that didn't matter, but I *knew* I was right, so I couldn't let it go. "No! That happened five years ago, not three!"

There's a famous story about two people enjoying each other's company as they take a walk in the woods. It's a lovely day, and they're having a wonderful time. Then they hear *Quack! Quack!*

One friend says, "That's a chicken." The other scoffs and says, "No! That's a duck. Don't you know the difference?" They keep walking, but their fun has been subdued. Then the sound comes again. *Quack! Quack!* "That definitely sounds like a chicken," one friend says, scowling. "You must be crazy!" the other replies. "That doesn't sound anything like a chicken!"

The arguing continues until there are tears and hurt feelings. Finally, one of them realizes how the disagreement is ruining their walk and harming their relationship and says, "I'm sorry. You must be right. That must be a chicken."

Harmony is restored, and they continue their walk.

Of course, there *are* times it's important to correct misinformation to avoid danger or making the wrong decision. But when it truly doesn't matter, can you let it go? It can be very difficult and goes against our instinct to be right. But if it can avoid hurt feelings or damaged relationships, isn't it worth it? Not only will the other person like you more, but you'll be happier, too! You might even find out later that *you* were the one who was wrong.

Think of a time when you argued your point, even though it didn't matter. What could you have done and said differently? How would it have changed the outcome of the interaction?

_____

_____

_____

_____

_____

_____

_____

_____

_____

_____

_____

_____

_____

_____

_____

_____

_____

_____

_____

# 68. Be a Bucket Filler
*The power of positive interactions*

Have you ever read the children's book *Have You Filled a Bucket Today?* by Carol McCloud?[56] It describes how we all have invisible buckets we carry around with us. Our interactions with people can fill or empty our buckets and the buckets of others. It's a wonderful metaphor illustrating how we feel happier and make others feel better (full buckets) when we express and experience kindness, appreciation, and love. We empty our buckets and the buckets of others (feel worse) when we have interactions that are impatient, nagging, or inconsiderate.

Research takes this a step further, showing that if we dip into a bucket with a negative interaction, it takes more than one ladle full of kindness to replace it. In fact, studies have shown that it takes five positive experiences for every negative one to keep a healthy relationship with others such as our kids, coworkers, and partner.[57] It's important to remember that the *perception* of the interaction as good or bad by the other person is what matters. Not our intention.

I try to remember this with my daughter. Sometimes I feel like she has the definition of "hurry up" backward. "I told you to get dressed. What have you been doing for the past five minutes? We're going to be late!" She prefers a leisurely pace and doesn't fully appreciate how fast five minutes can go by. Am I then filling her bucket with enough appreciation and love to replace the nagging and impatience? I hope so, but some days are hard.

At work, there can be an expectation that everyone is supposed to do their jobs without anyone saying thanks. After all, that's why we get paid. But if we want more effective teams and more productive meetings, we need to balance the demands and criticisms with more appreciation and consideration.

What about your relationships? Think of a specific example and reflect on the number of times you fill and empty their bucket. What are some ways you can fill it more?

_____

_____

_____

_____

_____

_____

_____

_____

_____

_____

_____

_____

_____

_____

_____

_____

_____

_____

_____

_____

_____

_____

_____

# 69. They Disagreed with My Idea!
## *Understanding differences in perspectives*

I remember having an interaction with someone that left me very frustrated and a little angry. I had presented an idea on how to improve one of our manufacturing processes along with my thoughtful reasoning for why it would work. They disagreed and waved away my reasoning as if it didn't matter. Of course, *I knew I was right,* but the situation didn't allow time for us to discuss it and dig deeper. It would have to wait until later.

I found myself replaying and ruminating on what they'd said and why they didn't like my idea. Wow—the negative thoughts were flowing! I knew this was normal and knew with a little time I'd regain my perspective, but for the moment, I was totally focused on what I *didn't* like. (Note: This is not a good time to make decisions or maybe even approach the other person.)

By the next day, I could see that this person who didn't like my idea had a very different perspective than me. They had different past experiences around this process and a very different personality. I also talked to a friend who was able to point out some other reasons why this person hadn't liked my idea that I'd missed. What a difference a day can make! I was now re-thinking my approach and how I could modify it with the other person's preferences in mind.

What a great reminder that we each have our own unique perspective that's influenced by many things such as our life experiences, values, personality, and thoughts (see Tip 55). When we can start to understand why we see things differently, we can begin to appreciate these differences and create more effective interactions.

Think of a time when you were frustrated because someone disagreed with your idea. Would it have been helpful to try to consider their perspective? How would this have changed the interaction?

# 70. One Look at Her Told Me to Stay Away
## *The impact of first impressions*

As part of my certification in Positive Psychology, the entire class from all over the world met for an in-person, week-long training in Massachusetts. It was amazing in many ways. The students were incredibly friendly, enthusiastic, and inspiring.

So when I saw Sherry (not her real name), she really stood out. Sherry was always scowling. She had a deep, furrowed brow without a hint of a smile. One look from her and I had a strong gut reaction. *Stay away from her! Boy, she definitely needs this positivity stuff! She looks very grumpy.*

As luck would have it, I was put in a small group activity with Sherry. You can probably guess that I was *not* looking forward to it. But as our group started interacting, I quickly changed my mind about Sherry. She wasn't grumpy at all! I was shocked to find out she was very nice and fun to talk to. I even saw her smile!

Isn't it funny how we can judge people instantly based on things like their expression? I wonder if Sherry even knew the signals she was giving off by her perpetual scowl. I wonder how many other people I've encountered in my life that I avoided because I assumed they were unpleasant based on their expression. I wonder if people have ever made a similar judgment about *me* because of a frown I had.

My interactions with Sherry reminded me of two lessons:

- Be more open-minded about my first impressions of others.
- Be aware of the expression others see on my face.

Now, when I'm at a meeting or just mixing with a group of people, I consciously try to keep a slight smile on my lips because I want to appear approachable. What's your "neutral" expression? Does it make you look friendly or make people want to stay away?

Think of a time when your first impression of someone impacted how you interacted with or avoided them. Spend some time this week noticing your first reaction to people you see based on their expression.

_____

_____

_____

_____

_____

_____

_____

_____

_____

_____

_____

_____

_____

_____

_____

_____

_____

_____

_____

_____

# 71. Positivity for the Greater Good
*Your emotions affect those around you*

D o you brighten a room when you enter or when you leave? I really like this phrase! It's a great reminder that our attitudes and emotions have a strong influence on the people around us. Most of my tips focus on how we, as individuals, benefit when we practice being more positive. Another very important result that we seldom hear about is the effect that our increased positivity has on our family, coworkers, and community. If you supervise or lead others, your emotions have an even stronger impact on the emotions of these people.

Think back to the last time you were around a person or group of people who were complaining or grumpy. How did being with them make you feel? Compare that to a time when you were hanging out with someone who was upbeat or enthusiastic. Then consider, what emotional influence were *you* having on *them?*

Scientists call it "emotional contagion"—the idea that humans synchronize their emotions with the emotions of those around them, whether consciously or unconsciously. Research indicates this phenomenon is partly due to an interconnected network of cells in the brain that make up the Mirror Neuron System (MNS). This synchronization is based on the details of people's facial expressions, body language, pupil movements, and even vocal tones.[58]

Here's an example of an amazing study.[59] Participants were shown a face with either a happy, angry, or neutral expression, but only for 30 milliseconds. The expressions weren't on the screen long enough for the participants to notice, so they had no idea that they were being subconsciously exposed to them. Still, the participants who were shown the happy face displayed increased electrical activity in the muscles used to smile and mimic that face, and vice versa with the angry face. The takeaway is that emotional contagion can be very fast!

What can we learn from this? Our efforts to get better at noticing the good around us are not only an investment in our own wellbeing, but also in the wellbeing of our family, colleagues, and friends. Because our positivity can affect those around us, there's a domino effect that spreads to our teams, departments, families, and communities. You have more influence than you know!

How can you take advantage of this phenomenon in your own life? Where could it have the biggest impact?

_____

_____

_____

_____

_____

_____

_____

_____

_____

_____

_____

_____

_____

_____

_____

# 72. Would You Just Listen?
*Knowing when not to offer advice*

Have you ever been super upset about something and just wanted to vent to someone, but then instead of listening, they start offering advice, another point of view, or a way to see the bright side? They don't seem to understand that their comments are *not* what you need from them right then. You just need them to listen. I'm guilty. I admit I commonly step into the role of offering advice or trying to point out the positive. However, there've been times when I was the person who just wanted to be heard, so I get it. When we're in the midst of emotional drama, we don't want to reason or analyze. We just want to express ourselves and know that someone cares.

One night when my daughter was 8, she couldn't get to sleep. When I'd tucked her in, I'd been on a teleconference, so we hadn't done our normal bedtime rituals. I soon found out that this was unsatisfactory to her! She was crying and telling me how I never spent enough time with her and how it felt like I didn't love her as much as I loved my business.

*What?!* My instant reaction was to defend myself—to tell her that she gets more of my attention and more opportunities to do things with me since I have the flexibility of working from home. That's when a little voice in my head reminded me—*she just wants to be heard and to know that I care how she feels.* Somehow I managed to fight back the instinct to argue and carefully listened and nodded. It wasn't easy, but it definitely made her feel better, and actually, I felt better too.

The next time you're about to offer advice or point out another perspective to someone who's venting, ask yourself, *What do they really need from me right now? Do they just want to me to listen?* It can be helpful to directly ask them if they want your advice or not.

Reflect on a time when you just wanted to vent, and others were intent on fixing your problem instead of just listening. How did it make you feel? Consider telling the other person that you just want them to listen. Can you remember times when someone probably just wanted you to listen?

*Section 4:*

---

# CREATING
# POSITIVE
# GOALS

# 73. Choose Meaningful Personal Goals
*Designing the life you really want*

Studies show that about 50% of Americans make New Year's resolutions. Six months later, only about half of them are still sticking to their goals. Long term success is achieved by 10%–20% of people, depending on which study you look at.[60] If our chances of success are so low, why should we even bother?

Whether it's New Year's resolutions or any objective we set, the act of setting goals gives us direction and focus. This makes us feel more in control, even if we don't fully achieve them. When we feel in control, we feel happier. As motivational speaker and author Brian Tracy said, "Goals allow you to control the direction of change in your favor."

Without goals, we can have a very busy life doing a lot of things we think we *should* do. But are they the things we *want* to do and are they helping create the life we want to live? There's so much to do and experience in this life. We need a plan so we can achieve and experience those things that are important to us. When you take the time to choose the right goals, you are intentionally designing your life. Our goals guide our choices and, as motivational speaker and author Wayne Dyer said, "Our lives are a sum total of the choices we have made."

One problem we face is that we commonly choose our goals based on "shoulds." We feel we "should" lose weight, "should" eat healthier, "should" go back to school, "should" spend less money, or "should" exercise more. This pressure comes from everywhere—our friends, family, commercials, social media, our inner critic, etc. Our goals feel like heavy obligations instead of challenges that excite us.

What if, instead, we chose goals that helped us create the life we want by clarifying the desires floating in our minds (see Tip 80)? These types of goals would ensure that we're channeling our time, energy and efforts into things that truly matter to us.

Reflect on the kind of life you want. Which goals can you set to help you achieve it?

_____

_____

_____

_____

_____

_____

_____

_____

_____

_____

_____

_____

_____

_____

_____

_____

_____

_____

_____

_____

# 74. The Wrong Reasons to Keep Going
*Designing the life you really want*

We hear a lot about the importance of grit and perseverance (see Tip 75). Does that mean we should *never* give up on our goals?

Actually, there are important indicators that tell us it is time to quit or at least change our goals. Consider the following situations:

- The main reason you keep going is because of the time, money, or effort you've already invested. We commonly call this sunk cost. It can be a common mistake in businesses and also in our personal or career goals. Maybe you've earned your degree in accounting, but now that you've spent time in a couple of different jobs, you realize that the day-to-day life of an accountant is not a good fit for you. Instead of dwelling on the past, it's helpful to listen to your inner voice telling you it's time to pursue something that will bring you more joy and fulfillment.

- The motivation to reach your goal has changed. If something in your life or work has changed and the purpose of your goal no longer applies, you may need to re-evaluate. When I was a scientist in a biotechnology company, I had a goal to learn all I could about nuclear receptors—a common target for drug discovery. After I was laid off and decided to switch careers, that goal wasn't going to help me teach people about positivity. Instead, I took the opportunity to choose goals related to my new passion of Positive Psychology.

- Your enthusiasm for reaching the goal has disappeared. This is more than short-term discouragement. The vision and passion that you had are gone. Maybe you were really excited to learn to play guitar because a friend was starting to take lessons and you talked about how fun it would be to jam together. After taking lessons for a couple of months, you just can't muster the motivation to practice. It may be time to find a new pastime that gets you excited in this present moment.

- You realize the goal doesn't match your strengths, and you should invest your energy in something you're better at. This can happen after you start a goal and learn more about yourself in the process. Maybe you learn that being an accountant isn't a good fit because you find you don't have the necessary attention to detail. Instead, you discover that you have a talent for seeing the big picture, a desirable trait for other professions.

If something isn't working out as expected, we have the power to tweak, significantly change or completely eliminate a goal, even if it's one we've had a long time. Our goals should be designed to serve us, not to limit us or to make our lives difficult.

Reflect on your current goals. Do they still serve their purpose? Should they be tweaked, changed or eliminated?

_____

_____

_____

_____

_____

_____

_____

_____

_____

_____

_____

_____

_____

# 75. Grow Your Grit for More Success
*Developing the trait that takes you places*

Why are some people more successful than others? Intuitively, we may think it's because they're smarter or more talented. Sure, these can be important ingredients, but not if the most critical component is missing. What is it? According to recent studies by psychologist Angela Duckworth, the best predictor of success is grit—the ability to pursue long-term goals with passion and perseverance.[61]

Research shows that grit is a better predictor of success than IQ or ability. One study found that grit is a much better indicator than SAT scores or physical fitness in determining whether first-year cadets will drop out of West Point Academy. It can also predict retention in the US Special Forces and retention of sales people in real estate.

When I decided to quit my job so I could go to graduate school and earn my Ph.D., it had been five years since I'd cracked open a textbook or taken an exam. I not only had to remember how to study, but I also had to relearn everything I'd forgotten in those five years and prepare myself to take four entrance exams. What kept me going? It turns out I was fortunate to have some key components that boosted my grit:[62]

- **Self-perception:** I didn't think of myself as a quitter, and I believed I could do this.

- **Social support:** I had great support from family and colleagues.

- **Optimism:** When projects didn't work, I would get frustrated, but I viewed these setbacks as temporary and part of the process.

- **Passion:** Getting my doctorate was very important to me because I knew I needed it to get the kind of job that would challenge me and keep me engaged.

Other components include:

- **Willpower:** having self-control over our behavior, emotions, and impulses in the face of momentary temptations or diversions

- **Resilience:** the ability to bounce back when things get tough

- **Growth mindset:** believing we can improve our talents and abilities with practice and hard work versus thinking our abilities are set

Reflect on a time in your life when you were pursuing a long-term goal. What kept you going? How can you use those things to help you work on and achieve a current goal? What components of grit could you work on?

_____

_____

_____

_____

_____

_____

_____

_____

_____

_____

_____

_____

_____

_____

_____

# 76. Don't 'Should' on Yourself
## *Pursuing the life you truly want*

Are you *shoulding* on yourself? Are your dreams, goals, and the way you live your daily life honestly your choices? Or are they things you think you should be doing and pursuing? Sometimes it's hard to tell the difference because we're so used to doing what we think is expected of us. And it can be scary to break from the norm and take our own path. What if others in our lives don't approve? "Yet, if we are always trying to be 'normal,' we'll never know how amazing we can be."—Maya Angelou.

These expectations and fears are less of an issue for some people than for others. But for those of us "people pleasers" (you know who you are), shoulding can be a major obstacle. We need to politely say, "Thank you very much for your advice, your suggestions, your ideas, but this is my life and my dreams, not yours." We might say this to another person or even silently to our own internal voice.

It's interesting that other people don't even have to tell us their opinions to influence our decisions. All we have to do is *imagine* what they're thinking. Many of our biggest shoulds are those we create in our own minds.

For example, I can imagine certain family or friends thinking I should have pursued another job as a scientist in biotechnology instead of reinventing myself as a speaker and starting my own company. I can imagine they thought it was too risky with too many unknowns, and it didn't make sense when I could have a job with a stable income and health insurance. I could easily let these imagined opinions influence my choices, so I have to remind myself that I need to be sure my decisions align with *my* priorities and dreams.

I've noticed that shoulding doesn't just happen in the work part of my life.

It also shows up in the financial, spiritual, family, and health areas. When something doesn't feel right in one of these areas, it's a good idea to ask myself if it's because I'm struggling with a should.

Take a moment to reflect on the different parts of your life. Do you notice any shoulds that get in the way of your dreams or the life you want? What needs to change? Who do you need to tell, "Thank you very much for your advice, but this is my life and my dreams, not yours?"

---
---
---
---
---
---
---
---
---
---
---
---
---
---
---
---
---
---
---

# 77. The Secret Formula for Success
*Leveraging passion against perceived effort to achieve goals*

Goals that require us to change are notoriously tough to keep. Whether we're trying to eat healthier, exercise more, get more organized, or quit smoking, the odds are usually against us. Unless . . . we know the secret formula for success.[63]

$$\frac{\text{PASSION}}{\text{PERCEIVED EFFORT}} = \text{CHANCE OF SUCCESS}$$

This formula can help you figure out your chance of success for a particular goal. The first step is to rate how much *passion* you have for making the change on a scale of one to ten, where one is no passion and ten is a huge amount of passion. Then rate how *difficult* you think it's going to be to make this change where one is easy, and ten is very difficult. Next, divide your passion rating by your perceived effort rating to get a sense of how likely you will succeed at this goal. If the resulting number is around one, success is possible but not easy. If the number is much less than one, your chances are very low, while a number much greater than one means your chances of achieving your goal are very high. What's truly helpful about knowing this formula is the ability to improve your odds by finding ways to increase your passion and decrease your perceived effort.

For example, you could increase your passion by considering why it's important to you to make this change. What are the benefits? The best reasons are not necessarily *shoulds* (see Tip 76), like "I should exercise more so I can be healthier." Rather, the reasons are emotional, "It's important to me to have enough energy to keep up with my kids (or grandkids) so we can have a closer relationship." Or "It's important to me to feel strong enough to keep doing the things I enjoy as I get older." Once you identify these more meaningful reasons, you can surround yourself with reminders about your "Why," especially in those places where you're most tempted to veer off course. The reminders can be pictures, quotes, a bracelet—anything that's easy to see that you associate with the reason for your change.

One way you could reduce your perceived effort is to use the 20-second rule. If it takes you less than 20 seconds to do the right thing, you're more likely to do it. For example, let's say you want a snack. If you can grab something healthy in less than 20 seconds instead of candy or cookies, you're more likely to take the faster, easier way. If you have your exercise clothes laid out by your bed to put on as soon as you get up, you're more likely to put them on and be ready to go. So set yourself up for success by making it easy and fast.

What is a goal of yours? How could you use the secret formula for success to increase your chances of achieving it?

_____

_____

_____

_____

_____

_____

_____

_____

_____

_____

_____

_____

# 78. A New Approach to Positive Affirmations
*Adding in the 'How' and 'Why'*

I've never been a big fan of positive affirmations. You know the ones—positive phrases you're supposed to repeat to yourself that describe how you want to think, feel, or act. The idea is that with repetition you start to believe them, and eventually they become a self-fulfilling prophecy. But it sounded too elusive to me. Then I read Hal Elrod's *Miracle Morning* book.[64] His take on positive affirmations really resonated with me, so I reconsidered.

With this new approach, I think about *how* I can achieve the desired outcome I'm committed to and *why* I want to achieve it. Here are a few examples of my current affirmations:

**Business**
- **How:** I prioritize my tasks each day and stay focused on those things that are the most urgent and that achieve my top 3-5 goals. As I start and stop activities throughout the day, I will ask myself if what I'm doing meets these criteria.

- **Why:** I do this to stay focused on what will drive the success of my business so I can help more people and enjoy a more sustainable and thriving business with less worry and stress.

**Family**
- **How:** I intentionally spend quality time with my family, remembering to be grateful for them, to build them up, and to show my appreciation.

- **Why:** I do this to build strong, healthy connections with them because my relationship with my family is so important to me.

*Balance*

- **How:** I adjust the amount of time and energy I give to the different areas of my life (work, family, physical, emotional, and spiritual health, etc.) as needed and am intentional and sensitive about the current situation of each one, recognizing that there will be constant fluctuation.

- **Why:** Living my life with balance between my work, my family, my physical, emotional, and spiritual health is important to my quality of life and overall happiness.

I definitely notice that saying these phrases out loud and focusing on their meaning and impact is important to genuinely feeling my "Why." Just as a reminder, these are a few examples of areas I'm *working* on. I do *not* have these perfected by any means!

Which areas of your life could use a little more attention? What positive affirmations could you design with a "How" and "Why" to try these next two weeks?

_____

_____

_____

_____

_____

_____

_____

_____

_____

_____

_____

## 79. Breaking Out of the 'Doing' Mentality
*Taking time to celebrate accomplishments*

I love to cross things off my to-do list. When I'm getting something done, it feels good. Like most of us, I've been taught that success comes from hard work. Our culture has a great disdain for laziness, which translates into "not doing." So as soon as I finish one thing, I'm impatient to start the next.

This "doing" mentality leaves no time for celebrating and savoring our accomplishments. It's ironic that taking a moment to reflect back on all the things we've done feels like a waste of time. Yet this reflection builds our confidence and recharges our batteries because we can see our progress. It increases our motivation to take on our next goal. Constantly *doing* without pausing to appreciate our accomplishments can drain our internal resources and hurt our productivity. It starts to feel like a non-stop cycle of busy-ness with no end in sight.

It's not intuitive. But if we want to sustainably achieve more, and not suffer from burnout and overwhelm, we need to pause and notice how far we've come. It doesn't have to be a major achievement—reflecting on our small wins is important, too. You can acknowledge finishing that book you've been reading, getting some paperwork done, making those phone calls, starting to learn something new like a different language or musical instrument. You get the idea.

At first, it may seem difficult to even remember our achievements—we're not used to noticing them. I know it's hard for me! It can be helpful to talk with a friend who can remind us of our progress. We can also keep a list that we add to as we think of more things we've done. We can share our list with friends and family and encourage them to do the same. Then we can celebrate together, for our own accomplishments and for theirs. Celebrating can take many forms, whether it's taking time to do something special, getting or giving something, or just congratulating each other. What a gift to help them remember and feel good about all that they've done, too!

Pause right now. What have you accomplished in the past 24 hours? In the past six months? How could you celebrate?

_____

_____

_____

_____

_____

_____

_____

_____

_____

_____

_____

_____

_____

_____

_____

_____

_____

_____

_____

# 80. Increase Your Quality of Life
*Aligning your goals with your true desires*

Did you make any New Year's resolutions this year or have you ever made a goal any time of year? If so, what was the purpose or reason for it? Common answers are, "I wanted to lose weight, manage my money better, get more organized, be healthier," etc. But are these actually the reasons for your goal?

If you have a goal for saving more money, to uncover the reason you could ask, "Why do I want to save more money?" Maybe it's because you want to buy something big, like a new car. Then ask, "Why do I want a new car?" Maybe it's because your old car isn't that reliable anymore. "Why do I want a more reliable car?" Maybe you're tired of worrying about getting stranded somewhere.

If we keep digging down into the "Why" of any goal, we'll likely find that the real reason is that we want a better life with less worry and more happiness. We think—or we've been told—that this change will make it better.

If the ultimate purpose of a resolution or goal is to increase the quality of your life, how would your choice of goals be affected if you started with this purpose in mind? Then you could look at your life and identify the one or two things you could do that would have the biggest impact. Is it really saving more money or losing weight? Maybe it is. But maybe it's something you haven't even considered as a goal before.

One approach is to look at the different areas of life and rate your *satisfaction* with and the *importance* of each one. Example areas could include your career, physical health, spirituality, self-growth and learning, fun and recreation, family and friends, partner and love, and finances. If you find that recreation has a low score, you might look for some ways to add more activities you enjoy. Depending on your interests, you might consider meeting with friends more often, joining a club around a common interest such as biking, or spending more time doing a favorite hobby.

What changes could you make in one or two areas of your life that would have the greatest impact? This exercise may help you identify one or two new goals.

_____

_____

_____

_____

_____

_____

_____

_____

_____

_____

_____

_____

_____

_____

_____

_____

_____

_____

# In Conclusion

Thank you for reading Sharpen Your Positive Edge. I hope you've enjoyed it and found some useful tips and ideas to help you create a more fulfilling life and work experience. In every moment, we have a choice. What do we choose to focus on and think about? It takes effort to override the strong negative bias of our brains, but the benefits are well worth it!

Try occasionally paging back through the thoughts and reflections you captured on the blank pages. Notice where and how your thinking has changed. What's different in your life now? Has your perspective shifted on any of the topics discussed? These pages can be a handy reference point to help you notice differences in your responses to life's ups and downs.

Please remember that positivity wears off. It's like brushing our teeth—we need to repeat regularly. So don't stop now. Keep going with generous helpings of positive nutrition for your mind!

- Sign up for my free video course, "Shifting into Positive Gear" at www.ThePositiveEdge.net/PositiveGear.

- Watch videos on The Positive Edge YouTube Channel at www.youtube.com/c/ThePositiveEdgeOrg.

- Get a weekly positivity tip delivered to your email inbox by signing up at www.ThePositiveEdge.net/blog. When you signup, you'll also be notified when I have new books, videos, and online courses available.

- Check out more resources like those listed at www.ThePositiveEdge.net/resources.

- Read more books like the ones recommended on the next page.

There are so many ways to access great information that reminds us that in every set of circumstances, we get to create our own experience.

Please consider helping to spread some positivity by letting other people know about this book. You could mention it on your social media posts or share a review on your favorite book website like Amazon or Goodreads. Thank you for your help!

There are several fantastic books related to Positive Psychology and choosing our thoughts. Here are just a few of my favorites to get you started.

**Recommended Books:**
- *The Happiness Advantage: The Seven Principles of Positive Psychology That Fuel Success and Performance at Work* by Shawn Achor

- *The How of Happiness: A New Approach to Getting the Life You Want* by Sonja Lyubomirsky

- *Positivity: Top-Notch Research Reveals the Upward Spiral That Will Change Your Life* by Barbara Fredrickson

- *Flourish: A Visionary New Understanding of Happiness and Well-being* by Martin Seligman

I would like to end with this thought—

What is the definition of true success? True success is not the money you earn or the things you own. True success is the emotions you feel every day. If you feel gratitude, serenity, and optimism, you are successful beyond measure.

# About the Author

Tina Hallis, Ph.D. is a scientist who decided to break away from her career of over 20 years in biotechnology to pursue a new path as a positivity speaker and trainer. Her discovery of Positive Psychology in 2011 motivated her to spread the word about this life changing science that helps people live their best, most meaningful lives. As part of her mission, she became certified in Positive Psychology through the WholeBeing Institute and founded her company, The Positive Edge. Tina now uses her scientific background to translate the research and studies in Positive Psychology so organizations and individuals can use it to achieve higher performance and greater success. Tina now shares her message with thousands of people through her programs, weekly positivity tips, and products.

For more details about Tina's speaking, training, and products, please visit **www.ThePositiveEdge.net** where you can also sign up to receive weekly positivity tips like the ones listed in this book.

# Notes

1   Two great reviews that include references to other books and papers on this topic are Shaffer, Joyce. "Neuroplasticity and Positive Psychology in Clinical Practice: A Review for Combined Benefits." *Psychology* 3, no. 12 (2012): 1110-1115 and Shaffer, Joyce. "Neuroplasticity and Clinical Practice: Building Brain Power for Health." *Frontiers in Psychology 7*, (2016): 1118.

2   This post on PsychologyToday.com has a nice summary of researchers and studies that focus on our brain's negative bias: Williams, Ray. "Are We Hardwired to Be Positive or Negative? On the capacity to emphasize the negative rather than the positive." Psychology Today. June 30, 2014. Accessed May 27, 2017. https://www.psychologytoday. com/blog/wired-success/201406/are-we-hardwired-be-positive-or-negative.

3   Lyubomirsky, Sonja, King, Laura, and Diener, Ed. "The Benefits of Frequent Positive Affect: Does Happiness Lead to Success?" *Psychological Bulletin* 131, no. 6 (2005): 803-855.

4   Gray, Kurt. "Paying It Forward: Generalized Reciprocity and the Limits of Generosity." *Journal of Experimental Psychology* 143, no. 1 (2014): 247-254.

5   Learn more in the paper Tsvetkova, Milena and Macy, Michael W. "The Social Contagion of Generosity." PLoS ONE 9, no. 2 (February 13, 2014). Accessed May 27, 2017. doi:10.1371/journal.pone.0087275.

6   Savoring has become an area of study within Positive Psychology with a number of scientific papers including Bryant, Fred B., Smart, Colette M., and King, Scott P. "Using the Past to Enhance the Present: Boosting

Happiness Through Positive Reminiscence." *Journal of Happiness Studies* 6, (2005): 227-260 and the book, Bryant, Fred and Veroff, Joseph. *Savoring, A New Model of Positive Experience*. Mahwah, NJ: Lawrence Erlbaum Associates, 2006.

7   The idea of a positivity ratio was first published by Marcial Losada and Barbara Fredrickson in 2005, but was later challenged by Nick Brown, Alan Sokal, and Harris Friedman. They disputed the mathematical analysis used to determine the ratio. In her response, Barbara Fredrickson cites many studies that suggest a positivity ratio of approximately 3:1 is common. Her response was published in the paper, Fredrickson, Barbara. "Updated Thinking on Positivity." *American Psychologist* 68, no. 9 (2013): 814-822.

8   Fredrickson, Barbara. *Positivity: Top-Notch Research Reveals the Upward Spiral That Will Change Your Life*. New York: Harmony, 2009.

9   There are many studies on the benefits of positive emotions. The following books talk about several of them; Achor, Shawn. *The Happiness Advantage: The Seven Principles of Positive Psychology That Fuel Success and Performance at Work*. New York: Crown Business, 2010, Seligman, Martin. *Flourish: A Visionary New Understanding of Happiness and Well-being*. New York: Free Press, 2011, and Fredrickson, Barbara. *Positivity: Top-Notch Research Reveals the Upward Spiral That Will Change Your Life*. New York: Harmony, 2009.

10   Fottrell, Quentin. "Americans Take Half of Their Paid Vacation, but Chinese Take Less." MarketWatch. September 11, 2015. Accessed May 27, 2017. http://www.marketwatch.com/story/americans-only-take-half-of-their-paid-vacation-2014-04-03.

11   Fisher, Anne. "Vacation Time: Why Don't Americans Take More Time Off?" Fortune.com. July 28, 2015. Accessed May 27, 2017. http://

fortune.com/2015/07/28/americans-vacation-use/.

12  Gump, Brooks B., and Matthews, Karen A. "Are Vacations Good for
    Your Health? The 9-Year Mortality Experience after the Multiple Risk
    Factor Intervention Trial." *Psychosomatic Medicine* 62, no. 5 (2000):
    608-612.

13  Wechsler, Michael E, et al. "Active Albuterol or Placebo, Sham
    Acupuncture, or No Intervention in Asthma." *The New England Journal
    of Medicine* 365, (2011): 119-126.

14  Moseley, J. Bruce, et al. "A Controlled Trial of Arthroscopic Surgery
    for Osteoarthritis of the Knee." *The New England Journal of Medicine*
    347, (2002): 81-88.

15  A helpful discussion of the placebo effect with a list of references is
    "Placebo Effect." American Cancer Society. April 10, 2015. Accessed
    May 27, 2017. https://www.cancer.org/treatment/treatments-and-side-
    effects/clinical-trials/placebo-effect.html.

16  Davidson, Richard. *The Emotional Life of Your Brain: How Its Unique
    Patterns Affect the Way You Think, Feel, and Live—and How You Can
    Change Them.* New York: Hudson Street Press, 2012.

17  A helpful article that highlights some of the studies related to priming
    is Margalit, Liraz. "Sensory Marketing: The Smell of Cinnamon
    That Made Me Buy." Psychology Today. January 20, 2017. Accessed
    May 27, 2017. https://www.psychologytoday.com/blog/behind-online-
    behavior/201701/sensory-marketing-the-smell-cinnamon-made-
    me-buy.

18  The following article does a great job of citing a number of studies
    related to the impact of clutter. "The Neuroscience Behind

Decluttering." VINAYA. November 19, 2014. Accessed May 27, 2017. https://www.vinaya.com/blog/how-changing-your-space-changes-your-mind.

[19] Martin Seligman discusses PERMA in his book, Seligman, Martin. *Flourish: A Visionary New Understanding of Happiness and Well-being.* New York: Free Press, 2011.

[20] In the following article, Robert Emmons summarizes the many benefits of gratitude from his decades of research. Emmons, Robert. "Why Gratitude Is Good." Greater Good Science Center. November 16, 2010. Accessed May 27, 2017. Another helpful reference is Emmons, Robert. "Gratitude as a Psychotherapeutic Intervention." *Journal of Clinical Psychology* 69, no. 8 (2013): 846-855.

[21] Alex Korb. *The Upward Spiral: Using Neuroscience to Reverse the Course of Depression, One Small Change at a Time.* Oakland: New Harbinger Publications, 2015.

[22] Nair, S. "Do slumped and upright postures affect stress responses? A randomized trial." *Health Psychology* 34, no. 6 (2015): 632-641.

[23] An article reviewing some of the current studies is "The Body-Mind Connection." Berkeley Wellness. June 24, 2014. Accessed May 27, 2017. http://www.berkeleywellness.com/healthy-mind/mind-body/article/body-mind-connection.

[24] Cuddy, Amy. *Presence: Bringing Your Boldest Self to Your Biggest Challenges.* New York: Little, Brown and Company, 2015.

[25] Many studies have been done related to the benefits of laughter. The following article has a nice summary of references. Sinatra, Stephen. "The Healing Power of Laughter." Heart MD Institute. 2010. Accessed

May 27, 2017. https://heartmdinstitute.com/stress-relief/healing-power-laughter/.

26  For a discussion and overview on personalized medicine, see the article "Personalized Medicine." U.S. News & World Report - Health. January 2011. Accessed May 27, 2017. http://health.usnews.com/health-conditions/cancer/personalized-medicine/overview.

27  A great article on recent discoveries in the area of personalized nutrition is Murphy, Kate. "A Personalized Diet, Better Suited to You." The New York Times - Well. January 11, 2016. Accessed May 27, 2017. https://well.blogs.nytimes.com/2016/01/11/a-personalized-diet-better-suited-to-you/?_r=0.

28  For in an in-depth review of different strategies and factors that impact the person-activity fit, check out Zolfagharifard, Reza. "12 Positive Psychology Interventions 3 Ways To Find The One You Need." Positive Psychology Program. February 24, 2017. Accessed May 27, 2017. https://positivepsychologyprogram.com/positive-psychology-interventions/.

29  Wolters Kluwer Health. "Giving support to others, not just receiving it, has beneficial effects." ScienceDaily. February 11, 2016. Accessed May 27, 2017. https://www.sciencedaily.com/releases/2016/02/160211184959.htm.

30  Thomas, Patricia A. "Is It Better to Give or to Receive? Social Support and the Well-being of Older Adults." The Journals of Gerontology. Series B, Psychological Sciences and Social Sciences 65B, no. 3 (2010): 351-357.

31  Amen, Daniel. Change Your Brain, Change Your Life: The Breakthrough Program for Conquering Anxiety, Depression, Obsessiveness, Anger, and Impulsiveness. New York: Harmony Books, 1998.

[32] Hutson, Matthew. "Beyond Happiness: The Upside of Feeling Down." Psychology Today. January 06, 2015. Accessed May 27, 2017. https://www.psychologytoday.com/articles/201501/beyond-happiness-the-upside-feeling-down.

[33] Rendon, Jim. *Upside: The New Science of Post-Traumatic Growth*. New York: Touchstone, 2015.

[34] One such study is discussed in Tedeschi, Richard and Calhoun, Lawrence. "Posttraumatic Growth: Conceptual Foundations and Empirical Evidence." *Psychological Inquiry* 15, no. 1 (2004): 1-18.

[35] Danhauer, Suzanne, et al. "Predictors of Posttraumatic Growth in Women with Breast Cancer." *Pscyho-Oncology* 22, no. 12 (2013): 2676-2683.

[36] The seminal paper that first introduces "The Broaden-and-Build Theory" of Positive Emotions is Fredrickson, Barbara. "The Role of Positive Emotions in Positive Psychology." *The American Psychologist* 56, no. 3 (2001): 218-226.

[37] Mininni, Darlene. *The Emotional Toolkit: Seven Power-Skills to Nail Your Bad Feelings*. New York: St. Martin's Press, 2005.

[38] Rick Hanson discusses these two modes in his book, Hanson, Rick. *Hardwiring Happiness: The New Brain Science of Contentment, Calm, and Confidence*. New York: Harmony, 2013.

[39] For more details, see Salleh, Mohd. Razali. "Life Event, Stress and Illness." *Malaysian Journal of Medical Sciences* 15, no. 4 (2008): 9-18 and Nagaraja, Archana S. "Why Stress Is Bad for Cancer Patients." *Journal of Clinical Investigation* 123, no. 2 (2013): 558-560.

40  Keller, Abiola et al. "Does the Perception That Stress Affects Health Matter? The Association with Health and Mortality." *Health Psychology: official journal of the Division of Health Psychology, American Psychological Association* 31, no. 5 (2012): 677–684.

41  Check out these two sources for more details; Jamieson, Jeremy P., Berry Mendes, Wendy, and Nock, Matthew K. "Improving Acute Stress Responses: The Power of Reappraisal" *Current Directions in Psychological Science* 22, no. 1 (2013): 51-56 and Torgovnick, Kate. "7 Ways Stress Does Your Mind and Body Good." TED Ideas. July 16, 2014. Accessed May 27, 2017. http://ideas.ted.com/7-ways-stress-does-your-mind-and-body-good/.

42  McGonigal, Kelly. "How to make stress your friend." TED talk. Filmed June 2013. Accessed May 27, 2017. https://www.ted.com/talks/kelly_mcgonigal_how_to_make_stress_your_friend.

43  Ellis A., Dryden W. *The Practice of Rational-Emotive Behavior Therapy.* New York: Springer Publishing Company, 1997.

44  Loehr, Jim and Schwartz, Tony. *The Power of Full Engagement, Managing Energy, Not Time, Is the Key to High Performance and Personal Renewal.* New York: Free Press, 2003.

45  The studies on fraternal and identical twins that help us understand the factors that impact our positivity are discussed in Lyubomirsky, Sonja. *The How of Happiness, A Scientific Approach to Getting the Life You Want.* New York: Penguin Press, 2008.

46  Lykken, David and Tellegen Auke. "Happiness Is a Stochastic Phenomenon." *Psychological Science* 7, no. 3 (1996): 186–189.

47  The two books I mentioned are Chapman, Gary. *The 5 Love Languages:*

*The Secret to Love that Lasts.* Chicago, IL: Northfield Publishing, 1992 and Chapman, Gary and White, Paul. *The 5 Languages of Appreciation in the Workplace: Empowering Organizations by Encouraging People.* Chicago, IL: Northfield Publishing, 2011.

[48] Rock, David. "SCARF: A Brain-Based Model for Collaborating with and Influencing Others." *NeuroLeadership Journal* 1, (2008): 1-8 and Rock, David. *Coaching with the Brain in Mind: Foundations for Practice.* Hoboken, NJ: John Wiley & Sons, 2009.

[49] For an academic perspective on the role genetics plays in personality, see the introduction in Krueger, Robert F. et al. "The Heritability of Personality Is Not Always 50%: Gene-Environment Interactions and Correlations between Personality and Parenting." *Journal of Personality* 76, no. 6 (2008): 1485-1521.

[50] Gable, Shelly, Gonzaga, Gian and Strachman, Amy. "Will You Be There for Me when Things Go Right? Supportive Responses to Positive Event Disclosures." *Journal of Personality and Social Psychology* 91, no. 5 (2006): 904-917.

[51] House, J.S., Landis, K.R. and Umberson, D. "Social Relationships and Health." *Science* 241, no. 241 (1988): 540-545.

[52] Holt-Lunstad, J., Smith, T.B. and Layton, J.B. "Social Relationships and Mortality Risk: A Meta-analytic Review." *PLoS Medicine* 7, no. 7 (2010): 1-20.

[53] One such study can be found in Pinquart, M. and Sorensen, S. "Influences of Socioeconomic Status, Social Network, and Competence on Subjective Well-Being in Later Life: A Meta-Analysis, Psychology and Aging." *Psychology and Aging* 15, no. 2 (2000): 187-224.

[54] An example of a study on this topic is Baumeister, R.F. and Leary, M.R. "The Need to Belong: Desire for Interpersonal Attachments as a Fundamental Human Motivation." *Psychological Bulletin* 117, no. 3 (1995): 497-529.

[55] This is one of my favorite books that everyone should have; Godwin, Alan. *How to Solve Your People Problems – Dealing with Your Difficult Relationships.* Eugene, OR: Harvest House Publishers, 2008.

[56] McCloud, Carol. *Have You Filled a Bucket Today? A Guide to Daily Happiness for Kids.* Northville, MI: Ferne Press, 2006.

[57] The suggested ratio of 5:1 is described in John Gottman's work with couples. See "Gottman Couples & Marital Therapy." Couples Training Institute. Accessed May 27, 2017. http://couplestraininginstitute.com/gottman-couples-and-marital-therapy/. The ratio is also discussed in the book, Rath, Tom and Clifton, Donald. *How Full Is Your Bucket?* New York: Gallup Press, 2004.

[58] Hatfield, Elaine et al. "New Perspectives on Emotional Contagion: A Review of Classic and Recent Research on Facial Mimicry and Contagion" *Interpersona* 8, no. 2 (2014): 159-179.

[59] Künecke, Janina et al. "Facial EMG Responses to Emotional Expressions Are Related to Emotion Perception Ability." *PLoS One* 9, no. 1 (2014): 1-10.

[60] A couple of sources for New Year's Resolution statistics include a survey conducted by Statistic Brain Research Institute, "New Years Resolution Statistics." Statistic Brain. January 04, 2017. Accessed May 27, 2017. http://www.statisticbrain.com/new-years-resolution-statistics/ and Norcross, J.C., Mrykalo, M.S. and Blagys, M.D. "Auld lang syne: Success Predictors, Change Processes, and Self-Reported Outcomes of New

Year's Resolvers and Nonresolvers." *Journal of Clinical Psychology* 58, no. 4 (2002): 397-405.

[61] For an overview of grit, check out the book, Duckworth, Angela. *Grit: The Power of Passion and Perseverance.* New York: Scribner, 2016.

[62] A number of articles relate to factors important for increasing our grit, including the following; "Do You Have Enough Grit?" Michelle McQuaid. January 21, 2017. Accessed May 27, 2017. http://www. michellemcquaid.com/grit/, Jain, Chaya and Apple, Daniel. "What Is Self-Growth?" *International Journal of Process Education 7*, no. 1 (2015), 41-52, and Hilmantel, Robin. "4 Signs You Have Grit." Motto. May 12, 2016. Accessed May 27, 2017. http://motto.time. com/4327035/4-signs-you-have-grit/.

[63] During my certification in Positive Psychology through the WholeBeing Insitute in 2013, our teacher, Tal Ben-Shahar, an author, consultant, and thought leader in Positive Psychology, talked about the science on the motivation to change and how we need an emotional reason to change (passion). Tal described motivation as passion/ perceived effort.

[64] Elrod, Hal. *The Miracle Morning: The Not-So-Obvious Secret Guaranteed to Transform Your Life - Before 8AM.* Los Angeles, CA: Hal Elrod International, 2012.